Wild Love

Wild Love

Kissed Into Consciousness

Dreaming-Bear Baraka Kanaan

iUniverse, Inc.
New York   Bloomington

Wild Love
Kissed Into Consciousness

iUniverse books may be ordered through booksellers or by contacting:

iUniverse
1663 Liberty Drive
Bloomington, IN 47403
www.iuniverse.com
1-800-Authors (1-800-288-4677)

ISBN: 978-1-4401-0089-5 (pbk)
ISBN: 978-1-4401-0090-1 (ebk)

Printed in the United States of America

iUniverse Rev. 10/17/08

Table of Contents

Prologue

It is my great joy to introduce you to *Wild Love*, this volume of ecstatic poetry by DreamingBear Baraka Kanaan. A true spoken word genius, DreamingBear is this generation's poet laureate of the heart. DreamingBear is a master of metaphor; "each molecule-mantra" tenderly kissing the soul's "supernova of senses." As you turn these pages, be prepared to be awakened as his eloquent and alluring words transport you to the "naked tenderness of truth" and the laughter and playfulness of "holy amorous mischief."

DreamingBear's spiritual DNA is powerful. A prodigy of Native American and Middle Eastern (Lebanese)decent, his ancestry illustrates a similar lineage with some of the worlds most profound poets: Gibran, Rumi, and Hafiz. Reminiscent of these poetic greats, DreamingBear's understanding of science and spirit as well as his deep attunement to the whispers of nature allow you to see yourself as Lover and Beloved, in universal Oneness.

Through his words we become enlightened, separation becomes an illusion, and a spiritual awakening unfolds. Our layers of identity, stories, victories, and laments to the Self that transcend personality disappear and we discover or our ultimate identity that is everyone and everything. Far from a state of self-delusion or escapism, this awakening represents the ultimate development of the most valuable qualities of human life: kindness, compassion, freedom, intelligence, and creativity.

Under DreamingBear's love spell, you will be ravished by "subatomic particles having a party" and will be moved to "undress your soul inside your heart's hallway." Together with DreamingBear we can end the emotional ignorance of the past and learn to treat each other and ourselves with greater dignity and understanding. His work deserves a wide and universal audience of not only poetry lovers, but also of life lovers everywhere. His vision is fully worthy of our cosmic status as spiritual beings in human form. *"Wild Love"* can uplift the human race into human grace, where we can live "the light of a billion suns" and "surrender everything to love" for "tonight we dance!"

- Harold Bloomfield, M.D., author of nineteen books including
The New York Times best-seller "How to Survive the Loss of a Love."

Dedication: These words are your own true voice, echoing of the beat of this heart. This volume is in its entirety, a romantic playful incantation to the Infinite Source of Existence, expressed here as Lover & Beloved who come together to form the One-Self seated in every heart, these love spells, are hints of my immortal affection for your every incarnation in all dimensions of the myriad seen & invisible worlds. My love for you is infinite, & everywhere.

~*Kissed Into Consciousness*~

There is a voice in the wilderness, deeply embedded in every aspect of nature. Once immersed there, the heart becomes capable of hearing what the universe is saying through the molecules on the wind, in the water, from the trees, within the fire, and in every particle and grain of this good green Earth. Most ancient tribal cultures knew & understood how to honor their existence through living in harmony with the natural world around them, & by merging perennial philosophical wisdom of the phenomenon realms passed down through epic oral traditions, with spiritual insights and applications intimated into practical understandings. What our ancestors knew, recent generations seem to have forgotten, that we are all natives to the Earth, we are all indigenous people to this planet, & as such, we each have an intrinsic connection & innate ability to be in tune to the articulations of nature. Science & religion are two pairs of lips expressing the same beautiful truths in seeming different languages, however to this vessel, the words: God, Divine Thought, Physical Universe, Time Space, Lover/Beloved, Source Energy, Existence, etc. are among the variety of culturally indicatory nomenclatures ascribed to humanity's ideas of omnipresence, omnipotence, or omniscience, & are thereby synonymous with that great uncharted zero point of plenum that is the stock essence from which all expressions in every dimension are exhaled & then cyclically reabsorbed.

The greatest teachers and therefore influences upon the quality of this soul & writings have been those mystic lovers of Oneness, who in their devotion to Truth & Divinity developed a body of universal adoration so encompassing, that it has spoken to the hearts of humanity ever since. This work is reminiscent of the epic love poems of Rumi, Kabir, Hafiz, & Gibran, whose understanding and appreciation of the One in All has had an undeniable and deeply evident effect upon the inspiration of this volume of love letters. This vessel also owes deep gratitude towards the innovative minds who have blazed new trails of thought inside old paradigmatic philosophies often at great peril to their lives, such as Copernicus, Galileo, Newton, Darwin, & Einstein. There are many perennial traditions which through threads of truth, have often prompted me into spiritual & intellectual ecstasy, however the afore mentioned are perhaps the most prominent of this pantheon of poets & new thinkers who by way of their authentic passion for being In love, have left an indelible effect upon this soul in its present manifestation.

Among the many gifts they gave, was an opportunity to explore unashamedly the possibility of the conceptual Universe as lover & beloved, as eternal parent & relative, as teacher & intimate friend. Though a student of every enlightened perspective & without preference to denominational texts, the present day articulations of religious & scientific perspectives are lacking in one essential ingredient, that being Laughter, or by way of extension playfulness and all the aspects of bewilderment that follow from the seeds of fascination. It is not enough to simply informationalize epiphany-experiences of the phenomenal worlds, when there is an underlying intuition, or feeling that begs to be known in a way that cannot be understood by the mind, only felt deeply in the heart. By heart, I do not only mean this palpitating mass within our solar plexus, rather the entire volume of the thoracic, which this vessel feels to be the nexus point of conscious awareness for our intersecting interdimensional selves, & which by definition contains five thousand times the electromagnetic carrying capacity of the brain.

Ancient & contemporary spiritual intellects knew more than the simple truth to which their authorship alludes, for within their romantic notions are double entendres and the entire veiled story of cosmological genesis. In truth, this world wants & needs to smile again, to laugh, dance, sing & cry without having to rationalize or theologize their emotions into doctrinal or categorical divisions. Existence desires inspiration for expansion, and an experience of the sublime in much same the way, as lovers want only to belong to their bliss. That is why for this vessel, consciousness begins with a kiss, the most tender, intuitive, and heart felt expression of affection given by way of our mouth where in we utter words into worlds, and can summon forth the latent potential of the Source plenum inherent in every quanta of our infinitude.

Finally, nature itself, the elegance & grace with which the universe operates from the subatomic world to the macro cosmic, is indeed a living poetry of sorts, and here in it is the intention of this Bear to give existence goose-bumps as it were, in the form of living a life of such beauty and authenticity that it makes God's toes curl with happiness at the sight of it, & to offer these words up as the living testament of what it means to be inherently embedded among the forest as a voice in the wilderness.

Love Spell 1
~Lovevolution~

The final frontier is not outer space, its inner space, and understanding the social lives of our subatomic particles by cultivating our consciousness like it were a crop. What happens when we combine the principles of the various scientific disciplines, biology, physics, astronomy, etc. and merge them with those of the inner world of spirituality, sociology, psychology, and then have the audacity to mix them together in the cauldron of mind & heart? A new worldview is born in the form of what I call: Love-volution. The antiquated evolutionary paradigm is predicated upon the adaptation of species to their environment through a process of selection characterized by the now famous idiom, "survival of the fittest" which really translates into, whoever is the meanest and most ferocious makes it out alive. If evolution is sustainable & taking place at all, then it must be taking place on every level of our existence, from the macro to the micro, the same may be said of consciousness, & it is also evident therefore that the world is ready for an evolution revolution of sorts.

This is where human development takes a quantum leap forward in the form of magnifying the electromagnetic volume of the heart space, and thereby increasing our innate internal capacity to care. In the new paradigm physical evolvement becomes almost secondary to the next phase of how we will adapt to our vibrational-environment, in the form of our ever-expanding consciousness. Proponents of the sinking ship of the past can jump on board this new streamlined vessel of thought as we rearticulate old words like "survival of the fittest" into a new modes of characterization such as: thriving of the kindest, where the brutality of competition is replaced with the tenderness of sharing an infinite resource for pure potential. If we cross apply

Lovevolution to everything that exists, we begin to see patterns emerge as one realizes that our universe is in a sort of continual metamorphosis, changing however slightly from one moment to the next, whether in extraneous energetic fields, or internal conscious ones. A Quantum Physics of the Heart might take the concept of evolution to a whole new place and see how on a sub-molecular level there is a conscious sort of chaos from which all of existence has emerged into the skin-thin 'genes' as it were of being made into awareness & form. We have as much in common with quasars as we do with monkeys, on an infinitesimal level at least, evidenced by the fundamental truth of Unity in quantum & spiritual principles. Perhaps it is also true that we have more in common with spatial bodies through a kind of emanation of awareness and intentional affect upon the universe.

In fact, we live in a multi-verse blooming with intersecting dimensional fields that operate in ways, which at the subatomic level seem to defy the very laws of physics. For too long science & spirituality have been opposite sides of the same coin tossed in a never-ending bet of who's right & who's wrong. What if we were to create a bridge of commonalities between worlds, take all the best parts of everything, and begin to look at ourselves as quantum beings that are in an experimental bio-suit of the body, which is always evolving into ever-expansive ways of interacting with the material & subtle energetic world. There is a new evolutionary paradigm blooming as a science of the heart wherein evolution is taken out of the laboratory of observable phenomena and into the arena of experiential happening, where our potential genius manifest as an Omni-awareness expressed within the zero point of each heart-space. Think about it like this, if our subatomic particles can flit into & out of dimensions, appear to be in more than one place simultaneously, and disobey almost every known law of physics, then doesn't it follow that we ourselves could potentially do the same? This is the beginning of the end for the old ways of thinking, being, & doing, because once we change the way the world feels about itself, things will never be the same.

Kamikaze Kissing Contest

Welcome to the tree of life,
let's climb the vines of each other's minds
& go out on a limb of love together
where we can more easily rub elbows with eternity
while we carve each other's names into a heart of light
etched from the funny bone of the moon.
One drink from this cup of destiny,
& you'll disappear with me into the mystery
of why our hearts refuse to be apart
& keep on sending each other love letters of light
in the form of falling-stars, fireflies,
& your smile to brighten the night
while our souls dance the hula-hoop
with the sparkling rings of Saturn.
When we kiss like this: wild & untamed
without a care of what anyone else in the world might think,
it's like having the divine audacity
to binge-drinking shot-glasses of 100 proof holy water
& let laughter be our cosmic chaser,
until we're drunk on darshan
& detached from every image or concept
which seeks to give Love a shape or form.
Play hooky from your have-to's,
you know you want to,
so take one more sip of these ruby red lips
& we'll become the voice of the wilderness
& the innocence of every creature
playing hide & seek with the One
behind the billion blazing suns pulsating
inside the indescribability of every movement of lip & tongue.
Quickly, while no one else is looking,
let's slip into the shadows of another dimension
where our day-dreams are making love to our fantasies
& giving birth to whole new realities
inside each breath & heartbeat.
A frontier of forgiveness
where your happiness is my Garden of Eden,

& the paradise of parted lips
is where we tongue-wrestle each other's tenderness
in the twilight of luminous fermented star-shine waterfalls,
whirlpooling their way into infinity's glowing giggling navel.
As a shameless display of my affection for you
I have spelled your essence in graffiti upon every cosmos
river tree & rock with the skill of an ancient artist.
For you, I have willingly leapt from the cliffs of consciousness
without a parachute of reason,
& dove face first into the event horizon of every black hole,
fishing for bits & pieces of forgotten truth,
& have fashioned them for you here
as the priceless jewelry of this golden honesty.
& now here I am upon bended knee proposing:
will you marry Freedom with me?
Come on, let's elope into ecstasy!
We can have a honeymoon on the visceral shores of Venus,
Complete with angel-winged excursions
into the mystic oasis of Mars.
Or better yet, let's have one more drink together
from this fountain of fascination
& become that sweet wine of intoxicating intimacy
that spikes the whole world's reservoirs
with equal parts of mischief & magic
until everyone is naked of the need to fit in
& entering themselves into marathon kamikaze kissing contests
where everyone wins in the end.
Because when we love each other without conditions
everyone wins in the end.
So come here you, come in close
& let's start a Lovevolution with our lips
& leave this shy world blushing with beauty
& drowning in the drink of a desire
to kiss this life like it were a love affair
& every being our beloved,
let's kiss this life like it were a love affair
& every being our beloved.

A Thousand Love-Letters of Light

My love for you is like this:
you feel lonely one night
& I show up at your Heart's door
bearing a bouquet of spiraling supernovas on a stem
& the entire Universe
which I have hidden in my Soul's shirt-sleeves
just to see you smile when I offer you a hand full of stars
& sweetly say:
~Surprise~

You say you're thirsty,
so I jump the fence of illusion
& end up in Heaven tickling God's feet with a fallen angel feather
so that her laughter & tears
will fall directly into your sacred parched mouth
so that you can drink freely from this fountain of forgiveness,
& taste first hand the living waters of the Friend.

You say you're bored
so I put my fingers of love together & whistle,
summoning a whirling dervish of Moons
who hand delivers us a pair of rambunctious wild giggling comets
as our personal escorts
through the undiscovered parts of the Universe.
Taking your Soul by its senses I say:
come Dear-One, come ride the winds with me!
Come feel what it's like to press your naked lips up against God's.

You say you desire truth,
so Dreaming-Bear hand writes you a thousand Love-Letters of Light
in which I spell out all of the divine details
of the Beloved's most treasured secret thoughts concerning you,
then come whisper them in your ear
in your wildest & most fantastic dreams.

What is your wish Sweet-One, tell me,
how can I serve you better, how can I be more generous?
Than to give you this tender-passionate-kiss
you've been wanting your whole life
than to offer your soul what it desires most,
to turn this tender amorous existence
into your playful dance partner,
& then to disappear in your heart
as a softly spoken prayer.

Cookie Jar of Stars

These words are a mirror reflecting your heart's truth,
which is tenderness, sweet indescribable beauty!
Last night as the Lover dreamt naked in a bed of stars,
half drunk on laughter & amorous with awareness,
I broke all the rules & read that divine diary
she keeps hidden under a certain loose enchanted floorboard
in the heart of your soul,
that will only open if kissed just right
with the seed syllables of light.
As I perused the pearls of your most pristine flower-petal-parts,
what were once great mysteries become infinite discoveries
as I marveled at the magic of your mischief making love to the moment,
& cried real tears for every wound inflicted upon our innocence
by a world without kind words
caught up in the cruelty of karma competitions,
where the winner is usually awarded
with an over inflated personality prize.
But you are a star whose light has foretold
the coming of the compassion constellation,
careful my dear, not to keep crucifying the Christ consciousness
that is resurrecting itself within you,
no need to betray your beauty or better judgment
with criticisms of others, doubts about yourself,
or by selling your soul to the slave masters of guilt, insecurity, & fear.
What the world needs & wants most
is for us to remove that victims crown of thorns from off our head,
& do away with all symbols of suffering
that tell an old uninspired story full of reasons
for why our fragile eggshell egos keep on finding fault in others,
& turning disappointments into reasons for being hurt.
What if I told you the Truth
the truth of what is really written in between the lines
on every page of Love's favorite footnotes for you,
the words: <u>Beautiful, Beautiful, Beautiful!</u>
With exclamation points & passionately underlined
in a frenzied fit of joy.

Now most nights I find myself making out madly with the moon
& writing the word: ~kindness~ into each holy kiss
wanting to so playfully tickle your passion to come out & play
with the page of your desire to be love without condition.
Not meaning to step on anyone's spiritual toes
the child of this poetry has broken that cookie jar of stars
you keep hidden in the closet of your consciousness,
along with wild innocent laughter,
& has spilled out all your sacred vulnerable divine essence
into the night's sky,
so that those lost in the darkness of feeling alone
might look to the moon
& see something of your sweet light essence
softly smiling back.

The Alchemy of Presence

Every molecule is a mantra,
each nerve ending a supernova of senses,
make all your investments in Love my Dear,
for her kiss is a treasure of rediscovering Eden.
Shooting stars are the after-effects of wild love-crazed comets
kicking up dust as they round the cheek of the earth
to catch a glimpse of your glory!
These words are my soul spilling over the edges
of my mind's body & onto this page,
filling your eyes up with light.
Come walk with me upon the Sea of Tranquility,
we can hold hands like lovers do,
fingers intertwined as we laugh & float our way
magically over the surface of the Moon.
This is my prayer to the Night,
~that we become One in our dreams
as stars blow kisses at us
from across the infinite innocence of endless discovery~
Raindrops are skydiving from their floating life as clouds
& falling face first into my sacred parched mouth,
mixing themselves in with the poetry & tenderness
of my tongue doing somersaults for you.
Right now, I am leaning my lips off this page
from across the distance of a millennium
coming in close to your ear
whispering these words with passionate intent saying:
~melt into me, let these two pounding heartbeats softly become One~
Tonight the sky is a slow-motion display
of the Universe breast-feeding on God's milk of light!
& everything in existence is licking their lips
to get a taste of this brand of divine madness
Here, I've bottled some of the Sun just for you,
when these luminous thoughts ferment in your heart's belly
everything will become wild holy laughter,
& you will keep seeing God dance so playfully with the Moment
& tenderly kissing the cheek of your Perceptions.
My soul keeps saying in the sweetest way:

~in this instant my Dear, in this alchemy of presence,
you & I are free to simply dissolve,
free to disappear into each molecule-mantra,
free to become One with Source
in this supernova of senses~

Playmates for Life

Before becoming intergalactic peace ambassadors,
we must first become internal peace ambassadors.
Truth is gracefully walking a tightrope of elegance between us,
while the Beloved plays peek-a-boo with existence
from behind an open secret artfully expressed
upon the stained-glass-windows of our eyes.
Like pilgrims discovering the promised land
of each other's milk & honey drenched laughter,
seeing every heart in existence as a star
undulating upon a midnight ocean,
& coming together as a constellation
kissing the cheek of innocence & saying:
you are so astonishingly beautiful!
Your tenderness is a playground
where these words become a merry-go-round of meaning,
down the super slide of sensations & being skin,
into a sandbox of pure imagination.
Let's leave behind the emotional-see-saw of up & down,
up & down until we're exhausted
leaving the bottoms of our souls sore.
Instead, come swing with me into the arms of eternity
& take a flying mid-air leap of faith
into the freedom & fascination
of diving face first into forgiveness
like a child runs into a backyard pile of flame-colored fall leaves!
Awaken your sleeping appetite for being amorous
& get naked with me in this honesty,
we can be like new-born-babies in a bubble bath of beauty,
knowing neither guilt nor shame,
only the purest parts of each other's flower petal hearts
blooming in divine holy mischief!
Our prayers are magic carpet rides for manifesting our dreams;
our dreams are the inter-dimensional doorways
through which our souls become the nexus point
for experiencing every possible version of reality.
There is no twelve-step program to practically achieving enlightenment,
no short-cut sure-fire solutions to be a so-called spiritual success.

Sure, social showmanship sells a lot of t-shirts,
but its authenticity that performs the true alchemy
of giving broken hearts back their song.
I wed myself to this innocence;
I marry my soul to the fascination of seeing the Beloved as everything!
Here I am again throwing pebbles of poetry
at your heart's bedroom window in the middle of the night saying:
come play with me!
I know you have to get up early in the morning,
but come play with me
I know your hesitation tells you that you shouldn't,
but come play with me
I know you have a million different excuses
for not coming out of your comfort zones to be wild & carefree
but COME PLAY WITH ME!
Forget every obligation care or concern in the world
that's keeping you from exploring the adventure
of your constant expansion.
The time for following in the footsteps of former avatars
& so-called ascended masters is over,
the time for following is over.
Why not now accept the invitation that the Guru
of your own glowing heart has sent you
in the form of an opportunity
to be a living embodiment of Source essence,
an infinite vessel for divine creativity!
Like a child-poet on the playgrounds of peace,
these words are my heart's tender intent
tapping your soul on the shoulder saying
hey beautiful, I've got a pocket full of planets & moons
that we can use to play a cosmic game of marbles.
What do you say?
Let's be playmates for life!

Love Junkie

Let's get high on what it means to be our higher self.
Because it's not about winning or losing;
it's about having as much fun as you can while you can,
that's why I always keep a flask of fermented happiness
inside my soul's shirtsleeves,
filled with quietly kissing quasars
and interstellar nebula in the nude,
so that someone thirsty for a dose of inspiration
can take a swig from these words of spiritual intoxication,
and be willing to leave behind every kind of constricted belief
that is no longer serving our enlightened expansion.
Welcome to Love's laboratory;
filled with boiling beakers of the boundless,
test tubes of tenderness and truth,
and the mad scientist of the heart,
making all kinds of mistakes and explosions
and then saying: WOW, let's do that again!
Let's have an experiment with mischief, and passion
in which we mix together all our sacred vulnerable parts
to see what kinds of altered states we can co-create.
Our hypothesis is this: If all druggies of divinity
jonesing for the pills of honesty
are given what they need,
then the certainty of each other's equality
will ultimately set us free.
You are a discovery on my heart's doorstep,
and I'm picking up the package of your smile
and shaking it to see what I can hear giggling inside,
undoing the ribbon of separation
keeping us from exploring one another's authenticity,
enjoying each and every eager inch of the mystery
dissolving into the discovery of your gift-wrapped innocence.
You've been holding back on me haven't you?
Well, the time for unleashing your intelligence has arrived,
because when you give in to the art of being untamed,
you are the poster child for satisfaction and freedom.
Wild and beautiful like that, you give this world permission

to break loose the reins of guilt & shame,
and quantum leap themselves forward
over the fence of small mindedness & limited thinking,
into a landscape language of luminous laughter.
& once you taste the wind again,
you'll never settle for being even a fraction less
than the most beautiful possible version of yourself.
So come ride the sky bareback with me,
and let's play a game of being the rain
and let our voices do aerial acrobatics
as the thunder and lightening.
What if I told you that I have found a way
to extract the pure distilled essence of every tear,
mix it with the alchemical agent of compassion in action
to produce a powerful hallucinogenic effect upon the ego,
wherein the veil of illusion all at once is lifted,
and the candle flame within you
rises as a firebird to become One Light with the sun.
You see, for me…
kindheartedness has become the super drug of the century
and as an unexpected side effect,
this cosmic feeling of bliss
has turned into an all out obsession with oneness,
and a new found interdependence
has transformed me into a certified love junkie!
I'm addicted to awareness
and its aphrodisiacal effect upon the mind
to develop a romantic fixation with imagination
and habit-forming friendships to fascination,
who's tender touch only fuels this love craving within.
Being nice is Nature's Narcotic,
and the whole world needs a dose of this medicine
to cure the ancient outbreak of cruelty brought
on by the dis-ease of neglect.
It's not enough to simply break the box,
when we've got such an amazing occasion
to be rid of attachments
to finite concepts of identity all together.
Some bend the rules, some break them,
& a fortunate few are lucky enough
to have found within themselves

a frontier of infatuation with their infinity,
in which each moment becomes an auspicious opportunity
to make out with possibility in public
the way young lovers do,
even when everyone is watching.
So let's get rich
in reasons for celebrating the beauty of what IS,
by giving away hits of our love
in exchange for heartfelt hugs,
until the whole world is high
on what it means to be our higher self.

The Tenderness Terrorist

Red Alert, Red Alert!
The tenderness terrorist is one the loose
& has planted a ticking time bomb of truth
in a secret somewhere hidden inside your heart's house
and is waiting for the right moment to detonate your devotion,
blow your mind away with beauty
& shatter all our illusions about love,
whilst the ego is searching frantically
under every cushion of comfort
& within the walls of reason
in hopes of defusing the explosive device of duality
which when triggered will incinerate your sense of separation
and utterly annihilate all our attachments to ideas of identity,
keeping us under the control of an occupying energy
which has us believing in the concoction of a competition of races
who may have many different hued faces
but whose heart's all beat to one rhythm
with the same color blood.
Meanwhile we exchange counterfeit currencies
in place of compassion,
& keep pointing unforgiving fingers
at our next door neighbors whose nationality & culture
could be cause for celebrations of diversity,
but instead becomes the butt of our jokes
and bullet fodder for the slingshot of stereotypes
that keeps breaking the windows of bewilderment
wherein are housed all our priceless treasures of togetherness.
But don't let them tame you
for you are an expression of love in time & space,
vibration dancing with sound swimming in music.
If you could pull back from existence far enough
you'd hear a song and the endless symphony of solar systems
would seem like a campfire
in the infinite emptiness of pure potential.
Because your navel is a portal to a parallel dimension
where universes collide in cosmic kisses
and supernova stars inseminate their luminous secrets

upon the pregnant pages pounding in the pulse of planets
pouring out vintage intoxicating skies
bottled with light & brewed in the beloved's own bathtub.
You see skin is our spirit singing softly
into the ears of eternity's longing for experience
as the myriad mystery of context texture and form
merging into the material manifestation
of your magnificence making itself known.
I could take a single sentence from your innocence
and string it across timelessness,
until the living water of your tears turns into a true love tidal wave
wiping out whole cities of critical thought
still embedded on the eastern seaboard of our enlightenment.
Because tonight the full moon is skydiving face first
into the eyes of the earth,
while our mischief is swinging from the stars
like they were monkey bars!
So let the spiritually insane
be committed to their religious institutions
while we run free hand in hand with galaxies
making love to our laughter in the glowing pools
of the shimmering oasis of your heart's greatness.
Let these words do a dervish on the dance floor
of your heart's appetite for happiness
and be absorbed into the inner space of the wonder-verse
that is awakening within you.
Wipe the seraphim from your once sleeping eyes
as we see beyond our sight & feel beyond our senses
all the sacred secrets open to reveal themselves
as a blooming billion flower petal lotus mandala
made of an endless infinitesimal architecture
of inter-dimensional root systems
that run like veins through stellar mating rituals
happening on the ceremonial stardust soil
of your soul's ancestral home.
Time to cut the umbilical cord to our past
of pretending and playing small,
for somewhere inside the cocktail of your consciousness
ancient lovers are pillow fighting with the clouds
and tossing chocolate covered comets
into each other's playful amorous mouths.

The final countdown has begun
this is the air raid bombing of beauty,
these words are weapons of mass creation
& your heart is ground zero
where ideas of inequality
and identifications with insecurities are incinerated,
as the old paradigm's self destruct mechanism gets triggered
by the fascination filled freedom fighter within you,
who is always dropping dirty bombs of divine inspiration
in the inner-city streets of your soul's imagination,
doing away with the word 'war' and instead
waging guerilla love-fare upon the foreign legions
of unforgiveness fundamentalism and fear,
who have infiltrated the Mecca
of our minds most holy shrines
and set up snipers of insensitivity
to the emotional needs of others.
Holding our happiness hostage
by playing target practice with being pretentious,
seeking to assassinate our awareness
by means of intercontinental ballistic belittling,
but you are impervious to the pathogens of patriarchal thinking
when you stop paying the overpriced rent of your attention
to the guilt guided opinions of others
whose judgments of you are really indications
of their own inability to fully accept themselves.
Because contrary to the political polls of others
there is no such thing as a war that can be justified
by simply labeling it with a brand name
& choosing to call it holy,
or a so-called righteous revolution
that has anything at all to do with giving in to the violence & cruelty.
So why allow the inherited feelings of jealously & rage
to form a consensus of dunces
that is quick to evolve into an organized oppression within you
which is always so eager to play the blame game
& declare jihad against your joy!
You see I've swallowed the keys of unconditional love,
so let's break out of this royal cage of perceptions & inhibition,
& become Oneness outlaws who refuse to be on the run
but instead stand our ground with gratitude

thankful for the gift of each other.
Knowing that the tenderness terrorist is on the loose
& that ticking time bomb of truth,
has just now gone off
in the form of you,
finally having the courage
to truly be YOU!

Love Factory

Let yourself be playfully innocent
without having to be spiritually or politically correct.
I want only for your heart to be happy,
& I know it will be once you reach within & gently untie your wings.
No matter what brand of religion we've experimented with
or what kinds of social contracts we've agreed to,
few things in this incarnation are as sacred & dear
as a sweet tender kiss & wild holy laughter!
Yet somewhere between history & herstory
there is still room for tears
rolling like a quiet warm waterfall
down the softly smiling cheek of innocence.
These words are a passport to other dimensions
where lovers are kissing naked on an infinite array of clouds,
& hand feeding each other stars as an aphrodisiac
to awaken awareness into being omni-amorous,
that is to say my dear, let's make love to existence
in the very way we live our life,
like passionate lovers in the heat of their desire
to dissolve into a hug-puddle of Oneness & softly become.
Let Dreaming-Bear break open that door of destiny
you keep under mental lock & key,
& out of your heart will come pouring naked giggling comets
& wild love-crazed angels
caught up in the divine rapture of their mid-air copulations!
Admit it! Somewhere inside you are always smiling
& eagerly rubbing your soul's hands together in anticipation
at the thought of a chance at being mischievous.
Just let the rogue sense of wonder within you come out
& flirt with fascination & freedom
in an around the world pilgrimage/adventure
of treating every heart in the universe as a shrine of our Beloved,
& bow in holy reverence kissing the soul's feet
of all that might have been neglected saying:
you are far more beautiful
than you've ever given yourself credit for,
& in this moment I pray you see the radiant splendor

of your own sacred burning heart.
In a world of seeming separation
there will always be the illusions of pain & suffering
in the form of fears & anxieties
about never quite being enough,
or cruel comments criticizing your unique expressions
of creative individuality,
but learn to let your heart be a Love Factory
that is always recycling broken dreams
& misplaced identities of "being somebody"
into a treasure chest of forgiveness
in the form of forgetting those lifetime achievement awards
at fitting in, & following all the rules,
corralling your wild untamed consciousness
from the infinite frontier landscapes of its unbounded nature,
to being held captive in a royal cage whose confines
you call your own personality & mind.
Untie this nightgown of truth
with the tenderness of your heart's teeth
& let's make love with our magnificence
until we dissolve completely together
into satisfied breaths of pure unadulterated bliss.

The Naked Tenderness of Truth

Let my heart be like the Wind,
free & untamed as these words reach in
& tickle your soft inner core with Light!
God is a tree & we are her many dancing leaves
breathing in the exhilaration & warmth
of a sudden-sweet summer's breeze.
Here I am again, milking golden honey from the heart of the Moon
& lacing the moment with wild wonder-filled laughter!
As I so tenderly cradle your soul in my palms
like a newborn angel of bewilderment & inspiration.
Now listen to what my heart, & an eagle's wings
are always saying to the sky
it is a one-word-prayer of: Grateful.
Today, the sunshine felt like Father's hugs, warm & tender,
as I dissolved into the sand being kissed by the sea.
The Night & the Moon were once such amorous lovers,
now they just wink & smile at each other
from across the waist of the Earth
hoping to catch a glimpse of the passion they once shared
when the universe wasn't looking
& they were free to simply dissolve into one another's stare.
No amount of searching outside oneself
can reveal the naked tenderness of Truth
which has undressed herself inside your heart's hallway
& keeps lustily whispering in your soul's ear saying:
~come kiss me, come kiss my sweet pursed lips in prayer~
Because Love is the softest realization
when it happens from within,
as you begin to sense & feel the sacred Beautiful One,
inhabiting every heartbeat & breath,
& every unutterable expression of existence
your essence & this world
have ever truly known.

Holy-Amorous-Mischief

Never trust someone who says: ~I love you, but~
for that's the kind of Lover who might not stick around
to catch you when you fall.
We were born naked onto the page of existence;
with nothing but the pen of our soul
to write ourselves into eternal ecstasy.
Sometimes, I wrestle God to the ground with laughter
& make her confess just how much she really loves Us.
Once, while the Beloved & I sat watching the Moon
chase the Sun in circles around the waist of the Earth,
she spilt (I think on purpose) a glass of galaxies
all over my Heart's pundit attire,
since then, stars fall from my every breath & heartbeat.

The Divine One is devious indeed,
often sticking her foot out when she sees me coming close
to one of her many hidden pools of Love
swirling in the eyes of everyone I meet.
& when I least expect it,
in the middle of crowds of conservative pilgrims,
she will sometimes de-pants me to my ankles from behind,
& run off giggling in Holy-Amorous-Mischief
leaving me to explain the most naked parts of my heart & soul.

Now, even now Pure-One,
the Lover is perched upon a hammock in your ear,
she softly sways from side to side
singing crazed-love-songs in your honor.
If you cannot hear her voice, I would say:
you needn't be so shy in the silence, you needn't be so shy in prayer…
for everything you could ever ask for, & all your heart desires most,
are having a sleep-over on a soft pile of blankets,
folded out on the bed of your tongue!
Just speak the name Dear-One,
just say out loud to your worst enemy the word: Love.

Never believe anyone who says: ~I love you, But~
for they are the ones who throw your Heart in the sky
& get distracted with your precious joy still in mid-air falling.
God keeps this world of beauty & brilliance
hanging from a string of Light tied to her soul's sweetest intent,
so that we can all be flung together in to the great Unknown.
I keep your tenderness tied tightly to the backbone of my inspiration,
so that if ever you should stumble in confusion or carelessness,
the softest parts of my poetry
will be there to break your fall.

When Angels Start Kissing

This is what happens when angels start kissing,
whole galaxies are born between your breath & heartbeat
& star-streams merge with giggling comets & rogue moons
to quietly dissolve & become One in the warm glowing oceans
sweetly smiling & softly spilling over the edge of your eyes!
Feathers start falling from the sky
as angels get amorous with each other on clouds
covered in illumined golden sunlight-honey.
Tell Dreaming-Bear where it hurts my dear,
show me where the world has wounded you the most,
& let the potency of these prayers
gently kiss over the fragility & misunderstanding
of forgetting that we are always One with Source.
In God's bathtub there are a billion-billion universes
inside each rainbow bubble
flirtatiously throbbing on the verge of being discovered
& popped open with wild holy laughter & starlight!
Disrobe your essence of the ego, or need to be right
to get naked with God & me in this hot spring of your heart
dive face first into the infinite womb of belonging with us
& your likely to become a love-crazed lunatic
whose lips are always ready for a communion candy kiss,
& wet with wonder as all your tears
merge into a chorus of tenderness
that is always singing so sweetly
into the ears of every broken heart saying:
~your salvation is already within you,
like a sleeping angel waiting to be awoke with a kiss~
See how the press of flesh becomes a prayer
as bodies come close like the palms of an impassioned pilgrim
discovering the promised land for the very first time.
Rustling wings & heavenly growls
when the Seraphim seduce the Sun to spread her sweet legs of light
while Venus makes out with the Earth
on a bed of supernova sapphire rose petals!
Let me tease the ends of your childhood to come out & play
with reckless self-abandon in this pinky promise poetry

Wild Love

I have hand written a thousand tiny kisses
for each inch of your soul's skin
which has been truly longing to erupt with utter ecstasy.
When the words: 'I love you' are sincerely spoken,
each moment becomes God's breath
blowing answered prayers to you upon the wind.
When angels start kissing, gravity stands on its head
just to catch a glimpse of what it means to belong,
Night falls in love with the Day
& Stars begin chasing Darkness to the edge of existence
where they make love on cliff peaks
of stellar nurseries & secret unexpecteds.
Then the Universe leans in
& begins playfully nibbling upon your ear whispering:
~you're beautiful my dear, so stunningly beautiful,
& I simply can't help but to always,
always be in-love with you~

Divine Wine Cellar

There is a secret closet in our Heart's house
where we keep all our unwanted emotional baggage
suitcases full of suffering, chests filled to the brim with insecurity,
vintage hand made bags stuffed with fear which we fashioned
with our own skilled-mind, to hold the most hurtful words & actions
committed upon us by someone in their great-loss-of-Light,
or their sad-imploded anger.
Sometimes, when the Ego is especially upset,
we take these bags out & threaten to leave the Lover,
back to the Hotel of Being Hurt
where the innkeeper rents rooms for the wounded Heart
to spend its final unforgiving days.
Your pain is ripe my Dear, Your pain is ripe
let it fall into the poetry of my palm.
Let Dreaming-Bear & happiness help you
clear out that hidden closet in your heart.
No more talk of "separation"
that mean old word gives you nightmares
then I have to come rushing to your bedside
with bowls full of prayer & drops of liquid-light
that I caught after tickling the Sun so hard
she burst into laughter & tears.
I know the sadness you feel when missing the naked press of Love
up against the indescribability of your own Soul,
because your shyness will not allow you to undress
your most vulnerable sacred hurting parts.
But Truth is such an understanding Lover,
infinitely patient & kind…
she always keeps her bedroom window cracked open,
incase you suddenly develop the courage in the middle of the night,
to climb in & curl up close in her covers of compassion.
& One kiss, just one kiss from the Lover's lips
is enough to have you giving birth to stars
& dancing toe-to-toe with the Sun!
Come Dear-One, its time for some internal self-renovation,
let's turn that empty closet in our heart into a Divine wine cellar,
where we can get drunk on bottled moments of awareness
& celebrate our union
with Love.

The Kissing-Christ

We're born 'loaded' & become poverty stricken through neglect,
Truth gives each of her Beloved's surprise custom-hand-made gifts,
in the form of a Soul full of color & Light!
Existence is an opportunity for artistic expression,
each moment, an invitation for creation in which,
Love is eagerly rubbing her hands together
in excited anticipation saying:
~Come on Dearest, open yourself up, & let's see what you've got!~
But if you never look Within,
how will you ever discover Who & What you really are?
Unwrap your Soul of the paper-thin illusion
separating you from the One,
just tear right through all the hesitation & small-talk today
that keeps us running in semantic-circles
second-guessing what name to call God,
rip off the ribbons like reasons for letting go of Love's leash,
so that the world may know the Light of your presence as Laughter.
But listen, Beauty's gifts are set to multiply once you've been opened
& the only way to stay poor in this insane-love-game with God,
is to Not give away your most precious parts of the Present
to someone in need.
Give your devotion away my Dear, give it all away for free,
without a thought of ever needing to get more in return.
For, why ransom cups-of-compassion to your most honored guests,
when there is an infinite well always overflowing in your Soul's basement?
Enough holy-wine for the whole hurting world
to have communion with the Kissing-Christ of your heart!
So now my Dear, take the Truth of these words
& let Dreaming-Bear's verse be the catalyst
that opens up your Soul's pockets,
& give, give, give this dry-world a drink
from the divine-depths
of your own gifted heart.

That Holy-Weeping-Altar

Here we are again, waiting for a moment that has just passed
come Dear-One, let me be your trembling-servant,
let me bow at your presence & kiss that holy-weeping-altar
you call your own two feet.
Let me offer prayers & poems upon the holy-ground of your Heart,
while I bring you bowls full of Light to fill your Soul's growling belly,
& wine-jugs overflowing with fermented-Laughter
to help swallow the moment down.
Conscious-creative-conversation
will become our daily holy communion,
the tender embrace & heartfelt kiss
will be our continual sacrificial offering,
we'll let each other's tenderness be our sweetest sacrament.
Your tears are my holy-water, your pain purifies these words,
& I come late at night to your bedside
to decorate your dreams with oversized candid-snapshots
of God dancing in your honor, & upon Your very tongue!
As if to say: don't you know
the Beloved inhabits our every sacred-breath!
You may not realize it yet, but at this very moment
there is an entire tribe of naked giggling angels
soaking in hot-springs in your navel,
they've disrobed their reverence
& whisper crazed-love poems
about their most intimate encounters with the Love
through overhearing prayers
you once uttered in your sleep as a child!
Here I am again,
pouring drops of the rainbow into the open wounds
of your sweet-tender (but still bleeding) heart,
wanting to so playfully remind you that all of Love's attributes
are sleeping within you, like children of Light
whose favorite form of nourishment is the nearness of your breath
against the Universe's softly-smiling cheek in Prayer.
Come Pure-One, come look into the mirror of Truth
& see your reflection in the eyes of Existence,
see yourself as you really are, a living embodiment of Love,

& then you will know why
why Dreaming-Bear longs to be your trembling-servant,
desires so eagerly to bow at your presence
& kiss that holy-weeping-altar
you call your own two feet.

Awakening The Sleeping Giants of Greatness

Fee fi fo fum,
I smell the blood of a blossoming generation of kings & queens
willing to be genuine in their generosity & do that which no one else has ever seen,
by personifying the positive energy of a self fulfilling inner-peace prophecy.
Time to spike the drink of this moment's punch bowl
with an irresistible urge to rise in love,
& wake the sleeping giant of greatness
within you from its summer of slumber,
because 99.9% of fulfilling your highest possible purpose & potential
is showing up and having the confidence to simply be your most sincere self.
When you smile like a Christ child in astounded astronomical amazement,
it opens the cosmic candy store door of your divinity
& let's our passion run in all wild eyed
& stuffing love laced libido lollipops into our already overflowing pants pockets
bursting at the seams with marshmallow moons and sparkling comet tail pixie sticks.
Right now I am swinging from a rope of light fastened tight with fascination
to the cumulus of your unconsciousness, weaving existence together
into a chandelier of new dimensions in reality with threads of truth
which have unraveled from the finely knit fabric
of our former freedom to completely be ourselves.
So let's uncork that catalyst keg of creativity & show the world what's possible
when we walk on the water of our fullness
& turn these living-words of rolling thunder
into the wine of celestial wonder & become so intellectually inebriated
on the intimacy of our infinity intertwined in a deeply romantic embrace
with our ability to embody our enthusiasm for living,
while the beloved transforms dandelion day dreams
into bioluminescent ice-cream covered in milky way whip cream,
topped with chocolate covered cherry flavored fire crackers of forgiveness
exploding in the mouth of the mystery's magic bean stalk of being free,
pouring interplanetary pop rocks of potency upon the pages of our playfulness picnic
of sharing these golden goose eggs of endless excitement
& crystalline cups of everlasting ecstasy
sweetened with the agave of psychotropic rainbow lit sugar cubes
inducing a sudden onset of acknowledging each other's authentic expressions
with absolute unapologetic joy.
Right now I am opening a worm hole of bewilderment

& willingness to surrender to your independent thought center's
overwhelming impulse of innocence to break through barriers of separation
do away with duality & boundaries of what we're "supposed" to be,
by lip locking eternity at the speed of love until the day undresses itself into darkness
& the sky gets drunk on cloud-cake & the amethyst ambrosia of time ripened sunshine,
then begins confessing her affection for us with exotic flowers
hand picked from intergalactic gardens
fashioned into extravagant floral arrangements of constellations
saying: for you I'd gamble everything without a thought of "win or lose"
grateful for the gift of having brushed wings with an angel.
Somewhere inside the globe theater of YOUR MIND
there is a Shakespeare of Quantum Physics,
who is always finding new ways to rearticulate lost narratives of who we really are
in this sacred science of the heart, whilst our childhoods are mooning each other
from across the equatorial hemline & giggling tummy of the Earth,
saying see if you can catch me in an extraterrestrial game of kiss tag
kicking up stellar dust on the astral planes
& causing holy havoc in the headquarters of the heart
as we shift our consciousness into the high gear of happiness
& hyper drive our individuality into being the hero of our own story,
where we can go skinny dipping in the oceans of opportunity
teaming with the tenderness of your tears
fermented into the currents of celebrating our pain
until it turns into an ultra-aquatic sea monkey
swinging from kelp vines in an underwater Atlantis,
filled with stunningly gorgeous phosphorescent mermaids
doing weightless Vedic yoga in slow motion, & giving your mind full body massages
in the manifestation parlor of making the world a better place,
in the form of living a life of such elegance & grace
that it liberates those around you,
by inviting the child within them to come out & play
with the purest parts of their personality that are still wild & undomesticated.
Oh let's be wild & undomesticated!
Just give yourself permission to climb this
Dreaming-Tree of transmutation with me
& we can make out with enchanted understandings of each other's unique qualities
in between sharing starberry bites of the night
and the perfectly aged vintage stash of northern lights, bottled Aurora Borealis
circa since before the beginning of time,
that the tipsy evolutionary Loveoholic revolutionary within you
has been waiting for the Beloved to break out.

Right now your molecules are making love to the splendor of what will be
in the bed boat gondola of gratitude
floating down the Nile River of nerve endings in your veins,
stretching through tundra's of harmonic frequency
where every atom, cell, and organ in your body is a mad-genius messiah
performing a million miniature miracles per second,
by way of keeping this bio-ship of the body going
through the Amazonian jungle of perpetuity
filled with culturally endangered species of people willing to truly be themselves
and fleeting memories of scenic split seconds
of you smiling & giving in to the glory of being guiltless & shame free.
So what ever damaged past-wounding debris we're carrying
don't you think its time to drop it off at the landfill of good reason?
Where emotional baggage & idealistic inconsistencies
are retranslated into the challenges we go through
so that we can have empathy for others when they're in the midst's
of shedding their old skins of inherited behaviors that no longer serve our vision
of radical nonviolence towards ourselves & each other.
Meanwhile your DNA is doin' a little dance makin' a little love,
and gettin' down tonight
on the revolving 5th dimensional discothèque
of this very moment of being reborn
in the birthing pools of our 15 billion year infancy,
springing from a single seed syllable of sound mouthed as Mother Nature
nurturing our every need by breastfeeding our body into being
& nourishing us in places that have never been touched before.
It's true, your essence inhabits a skin temple,
but it is also a theme park of pleasure
& sometimes it can even be a candlelit bedroom of brilliance
where all kinds of carnal desires of clarity and amorous appetites of awareness
go to satiate their hunger for experience & expansion,
so let's open our clown chakras shall we?
Which is located in the blood marrow of the funny bone,
because this is the part of the movie of your life, where the main character, YOU...
gives Fate a break from calling all the shots, & gets to sit in the director's seat
of your destiny's unscripted docudrama style love story
set to explore the skin-thin contrast between our immortal inner-energy
and the great uncharted nexus where all expressions of existence
merge into a single quintessence.
So let's layout without clothes on the shores of satisfaction
we can drink pina-colada coconut lilac coolers of contentment

and play in the tide pools of treating every being as our beloved,
taking it easy in the tropical paradise of tranquility,
because look, the universe has complimented our episodic adventure
with an all star cast of divine rascals
in the form of 8 billion human cousins & counting
and a whole host of extended earth family
swinging like the sweetest swollen fruit of discovery
from that fabled forbidden garden-variety 'knowledge of good & evil tree'
but there's no serpent of fear here,
just your own voice echoing off the beat of this heart,
so let yourself be naughty & have a little nibble,
because even a petite portion of the Oneness
will transport you to a fantasy island
of forgetting all your inconsistencies & so-called mistakes of the past,
because everything about you is beautiful, everything about you is beautiful
even the parts that are uncomfortable or in evolution,
& what you did or didn't do
is just the story that you've repeated to yourself & others for so long
that you slipped on the script being IT
& hit your heart's head hard on the floor of finding fault in others,
& forgot we are all really royalty
whose treasure isn't in a kingdom of possessing material things
but in sharing the wealth & riches of each other's unique company.
& I'm sorry to say that as a result of that cataclysmic loss of memory
serendipity stopped speaking when you ended up
believing your soul to be homeless
& began begging for change on the outskirts of enlightenment.
Wiping the windows of passing wonderist with a spiritual squeegee
hoping to catch a few common cents of the courage to be the inspiration you seek.
Holding up a cardboard sign on the side of the road of excuses that reads:
WHY ME?!?
But the magician within
has an experimental chemistry-set cure for this ancient amnesia,
& the futurist pharmacist foresees a full recovery,
after all laughter is the best medicine & this honesty is the remedy,
so just let the comedian of your skin come out & do a set of anecdote jokes
about not taking life so seriously when things don't seem to go your way
or others disagree with your transparency,
because your true self a.k.a. the Source of creation chuckles at the thought
of giving into guilt guided gossip of others by denying your birthright of boundlessness
in exchange for the supposed safety of following the Sheppard of society

into the package of prescribed behaviors like a sacrificial lamb,
but the black sheep within you is really a wild honey-bear in woolen pajamas
yawning off the sleeping pills of an illusion induced hibernation
& as always is willing to break a rule or two in the sweetest way,
especially when it comes to that which tradition deems strictly taboo,
like reaching outside of the ego to hug & heal a complete stranger
or responding to the careless condemnations of your internal ingenuity
without falling into the rabbit hole of addictions to anger
by remembering who you really are,
a living Loveolutionary legend on the loose leaving a trail of mended hearts
inside the last supper scene of every commune-ication
exchanged in this commerce of coequality where the currency is compassion
& the richest among us are those who recognize the essence of their loved ones
in the lingering looks on every face & can say & do for others
that which most would reserve for so-called friends & family,
or members of the right religion or political party
whose points of view are merely extensions of their parent's paradigm
passed on to them by the prehistoric predecessors
of the patriarchy's pointing finger policy.
Time to come out of the stone age concept
of declaring war against our preferred so-called enemy,
in-a-me, indicating that being quick to cast criticism
has a way of boomeranging,
& throwing verbal stones in an eye for eye tooth for tooth mentality
leaves the whole world feeling blind & toothless.
So let's take that malnourished refugee of fulfilling our life's dreams
out of the cages of reckless-neglect
& into this metamorphosis cocoon of reincarnation
to grow new wings & feed your soul the super food of personal power,
and begin rising into your fullness until the sleeping giant within you awakens
into the larger than life luminary whose living example of unconditional love
becomes a light source that helps the whole hurting world to see,
saying fee fi fo fum, I smell the blood of a blossoming generation of kings & queens
willing to be genuine in their generosity
& do that which no one else has ever seen,
by personifying the positive energy
of a self fulfilling inner-peace prophecy.

Dinner-date With Love

The Mind is addicted to forms & worrying about things
over which it has no control
while the Soul can be found tugging on the Heart's shirt sleeve
to whisper this secret in your ear:
~there is an undiscovered universe in here~
but the Mind doesn't listen, only tears itself apart
searching for tangible tenderness in imaginary truths.
Listen, if you let it, your Mind will crawl through city sewers
of waste-filled-thought
looking for Meaning in the least likely of places
& then climb back in bed still covered in grime-&-guilt,
without a care for your precious clean Pure-Heart
which has been softly dreaming within,
waiting to be awoke with a kiss
from the most pristine lips of utter Awareness.
Why keep your devotion hidden under a mattress
in a part of you that has the word ~Private~ posted,
next to a sign that reads: Keep Out!?
Why keep your divine gifts locked away in a dark room of neglect,
half-starved from being unshared,
don't you know dreams die like that?
Why keep following the child of your Mind into haunted alleys full of fear,
when your Spirit has a dinner-date to commune with Love?
Let your innocent-thoughts run free
upon the playgrounds of this potency,
while the Nameless part of you makes love to Source
in a bed of stars under covers of clouds.
Stop holding your heart hostage with talk of separation
tortuously withholding your touch
when the Lover offers you her most sacred parts in Prayer,
whispering this light in your ear:
~come Dear-One, come,
there is an unexplored universe inside you~

Tenderly Kissing all of Creation

Pain is the catalyst for compassion;
until you fully embrace your pain
you cannot truly embody compassion.
It's like standing on the edge of a cliff
& thinking out loud to yourself:
~what if I jump, I wonder if I'll rise~
The answer is YES
when you take a flying leap into the arms of Eternity
like a child jumping into their mother's arms,
you always get caught-up in holy rapture & ecstatic laughter.
True alchemy is being able to transform pain into beauty
your hurtful thoughts into light-filled prayers.
Because somewhere inside you
prophets are foretelling the future saying:
~we are as we think & feel ourselves to be~
But the Ego is an unbeliever in anything but itself
best to put that screaming child to sleep
before it runs up anymore debts at the bank of Oneness,
always taking for granted
that being an individual means being separate,
when we are but the many flames of a fire
stemming from one Light-Source,
all doing a different discovery-dance of brilliance & becoming
luminous beings of laughter & star-shine.
If you are lost my dear,
if you are feeling broken & alone,
then draw near to me;
let me spoon-feed you
my most tender intimate loving thoughts.
Let these words break into light
& flood your soul with happiness,
as you so gently become the One you've been looking for all along,
you ARE the One you've been needing your whole life.
Here I am again, saying with passionate playfulness:
~WOW & what a discovery you have become~
Just to see you smile like that, like children do
in absolute surrender to the freedom they feel inside,

when teasing the tickle-spot of the Tender-One
to come alive & dance inside their fear,
that's when the Truth turns into your tongue
& begins Tenderly Kissing all of creation whispering:
Pain is the catalyst for compassion,
until you fully embrace your pain
you cannot truly embody compassion.

The Flood of Laughter & Tears

In the interest of staying open,
I displayed my Heart in a prominent place in my life,
out in the accessibility of being known
I used to worry that it wasn't safe being so exposed,
I thought it might get broken in all the carelessness
& of course, it did.
Then, amidst all the confusion,
between the fear & pain,
as I mourned over the finality of being completely shattered
there, among the tattered remnants of my misunderstanding,
I discovered my heart within a heart, still beating…
& knew instantly, that even in the breaking,
I could only be broken-Open
Broken~   ~Open
Now when my Heart teeters on the edge of crashing,
& I feel my fears begin to rise
I remember that there is always another heart within
which can never be destroyed
a heart so swollen with significance
that it often explodes on its own,
just to drown itself in the flood of laughter & tears
which inevitably always follows.

The Loveicide Bomber

Viva la Lovevolution!
These love-letters have been laced with a lethal dose of light,
so that upon hearing these prayers your heartbeat & breath
will dissolve into infinitely expanding universes
of Quantum-conscious compassion-filled thought.
I'm a Loveicide bomber Beautiful,
& these love-spells are the instruments of apathy's inevitable demise.
I keep strapping Kamikaze kisses
to each tenderly exploding world I write,
& setting them off in overly crowded rooms
of unsuspecting spiritual & intellectual civilians
whose lives have grown dull with anticipation
& just in need of an unexpected & more than major-league-miracle
to reignite that passion powder-keg
whose fuse in you, even now is beginning to spark!
In the playgrounds & market places you'll find me
plotting trip-wires of laughter,
triggering the chemical chain reaction
that results in a catastrophically beautiful series
of sincere hugs, gestures of friendship, & the kinds of smiles
that always bespeak of absolute unconditional kindness!
Behind every altar of fear, & shrine of guilt
that our minds & this world have erected,
I have set up poetically timed detonations
of divine ego-destroying devices,
leaving our devotion free of the terrorizing-tendency
to ever try & role-play or pretend
that we're something less than we really are.
Deep within the infrastructure of every insecurity & fear;
which has been the result of believing in the illusion
that you are ever separate from Source,
I have planted incendiary incantations of illuminated love-letters
& volatile Molotov cocktails of sacred thought
filled with mating galaxies & softly exploding supernova lovers,
causing the entire empire of emptiness within each broken heart
to crumble & become free of the petty tyrannies
of holding preconceived notions
& fault filled judgments of anyone else for not fitting in,

by having the courage to sincerely be themselves.
Indeed in each cell & molecule
of every particle & wave across the entirety of existence,
I have set booby-traps of beauty
that transmute tears into tenderness,
turn darkness into light,
stories of tragedy into reasons for rising in love.
You're bound to be expanding with ecstasy my dear,
as you taste the flaming freedom-fruit
of the kissing prophet's God-wet-lips.
For you, I have tattooed Happiness upon the sky's lower back
with a pen made entirely of stars,
I have exchanged secrets with the moon
about the most intimate moments of your existence
& written the sweetest parts of your essence
upon every page lining the womb of infinite belonging.
In this sacred self-annihilation,
the "I" in 'me' has been blown into a billion-billion
un-nameable indistinguishable vulnerable throbbing parts,
& pieces of what I once thought to be merely Dreaming-Bear,
have now undressed themselves as the glowing embers
of your own dancing gypsy soul
which keeps re-emerging from the ashes
as the myriad re-evolution of faces & forms.
It's because of you, it's all your fault!
Because of you my dear,
these love spells have been laced with a lethal dose of light,
so that upon hearing these prayers
your heartbeat & breath will explode
into infinitely expanding universes
of Quantum-conscious compassion-filled thought.

A Tiny One-Person Bed

You & God are like two newly-weds
in a tiny one-person bed,
you keep waking yourself up
in the middle of the night (farting)
& God, not having the heart to see you embarrassed,
laughingly apologizes
& politely takes all the blame.

A Keg of Stars on Tap

In a world of Oneness there is no such thing as inequality…
like a lush for Love I always keep a keg of stars on tap
& will often pour out a glass of galaxies for wayward travelers,
as the Sky squeezes the last drops of liquid light
from the tender smile of the sun.
Right now I am spoon-feeding you baby bites of full-on-ness,
as we surf the sparkling waves along this ocean of understanding.
I see you've dropped your smile again,
let Dreaming-Bear dust it off for you
& re-adorn that masterpiece of magnificence
upon the soft throbbing innocence of this world's joy,
because I've been told by more than one recently mended heart,
that when you pull back the blushing red curtain of your lips
to reveal that choir of teeth all dressed in white robes
& dancing so playfully upon the altar of your tongue
it gives the shattered soul a reason to rise & be whole again!
A new day is dawning within you
as a living opportunity to be happy & carefree.
Today I laid myself out naked under the sky and said:
kiss me, every part, let my most sacred vulnerable essence
be consumed completely in the light,
& I've never felt more alive than I do right now,
in this very moment
as these words are reaching into your soft inner core
to embrace something beautiful within you
which has been neglected for so long
that you forgot you were once such an intimate lover with the One
who created every kind of kiss
upon each precious heart in all dimensions.
It doesn't matter what the rest of the world thinks of you
or of how much pain you've managed to store up
in that dark secret unnamable place,
for this sea of tears will soon turn into sweet living waters
once you take a drink of the milk & honey
of your own capacity for re-creation.
If you embrace me in this potency
our heartbeats will become our own private drum circle,

& you will soon discover in the secret chambers of this heart
a golden enchanted door which only you can enter,
upon it is written a jeweled inscription which reads:
There is always peace when we learn to love ourselves
& each other without shame.
If you knock, wanting to come inside
the door will open to reveal
that you already are & always have been
softly dreaming within me.
Stop being so hard on yourself,
maybe you're not perfect
& perhaps you never will be,
but even if you were, someone somewhere in this world
would still find a so-called good reason
to criticize your greatness with words of being small.
So let your heart be wild & free
& come fly with me upon the phoenix wings,
& let's dissolve together completely
into that conscious cloud of kisses
that is always saying in a sweet love language
what every heart & soul longs & needs to hear most,
words of: welcome home sweet angel,
welcome home.

The Love Bandit

It's about being who you really are in your highest potential,
& not who the world says you should be,
that's the truest form of self-expression!
From where I now exist I can see for eons in all directions,
the Universe is Love's bedroom,
this moment is her navel,
& we are the many kisses being planted upon the length of her skin
by the love-crazed soul of Existence.
What we call the Milky Way is but a drop of divinity
from our Beloved's beautiful blossoming breasts.
I can feel God trying on my body,
she wears me now like the Universe wears Time,
my eyes have become turquoise sparkling galaxies,
stars fall from my breath as words become worlds
& playfully dance-laugh-spin around the axis of your heart's Sun.
The Earth is a pearl-drop-tear escaping Heaven's own ecstasy
over being ravished by joy & holy bewilderment
at the innocence of what it means to exist inside You!
The stars are but our Lover's many fire-rose candles
that light the way as she get's up in the middle of the night
& goes to get a drink of other dimensions!
For you I have become a love bandit,
& can be found prowling with poetry in the night.
I keep plucking meteorite diamonds
from their invisible stems in the sky,
& bringing them to you as a blazing bouquet of cosmic carnations
that open to reveal their breathtaking beauty
to the fascination of your fully opened & formless First-Eye.
Your consciousness is a new born phoenix
rising from the ashes of awareness,
as atoms bear witness to your timelessness!
Meanwhile, existence keeps spreading her legs with laughter
to reveal all those wonderful secrets,
as I stand in awe of the comets that keep coming at me
from across the eternity of your smile.
The Moment is an invitation begging to be explored!
Our hearts are galactic butterflies dancing upon the wind & poet-trees.

These words are my arms & soul opening wide
to give the Universe a great big tender hug saying:
come here you, come in close & let the bear get his paws on ya!
When our souls kiss like this,
I can feel Love growling softly inside my belly saying:
you ARE home my dear,
Home IS You.
I can hear the Universe say:
you are My home,
& My home is inside you.

The Milky Way

In the milk of the moment
existence is a luminous butterfly made of sound & color
undulating in an infinite invisible language
of kindness & soft thought.
Just disrobe your mind of all concepts & forms
& dissolve with me into pure energy, pure essence, pure light.
Be free of attachments to identity as anything other than Source,
there is no need, there is no lack, no storyline to follow,
so just surrender to the serenity & sweet sensations
of the beautiful truth that you ARE!
What wonders have been written & woven
into the very fabric of consciousness
as tenderness turns into a tapestry of smiling galaxies
& intimately kissing stars!
We are the warmth between the Lover's lips
as eternity opens her mouth to let out a sweet sigh of:
oh my God-ness it feels so good to be alive!
Deep in this cosmic womb there are planets as poems
being recited into reality as ecstatic playful prayers
of what it means to finally become,
oh let's become laughter
exploding into the lives of being the Beloved
in so many beautiful expressions & embodiments of brilliance
making love to the page of unending possibility,
merging with manifestation in our very breath & heartbeat,
reveling in the bath of our soul's body
trying on one of its many skin-thin gowns.
There is no greater "truth" than this:
sweet undeniable tenderness
happening in every true lovers kiss
as we exchange drinks of Love
from the living-water-cup
of each other's always overflowing tongue.
I speak you into me as the one becoming two
becoming One again.
Inside this embrace,
in between our every thought image or misconception

there is the through line of loving
of being Love absolute & unconditional.
When all the emotional children have exhausted themselves
on the full spectrum between suffering & being joy,
after every inconceivable intention has made wanton love
with the wildest parts of Truth within themselves,
after every story has been lived, written, retold & then lived again
there will still just be the bliss of the Lover's ineffable kiss.
Right now, the Universe is opening
her beautiful blossoming breasts to you saying
welcome home dearest, welcome to the Milky-Way,
wrap your soul's mouth around these supple words
& drink as much as you wish,
knowing forever that you belong.

The Laughing Genie

I can feel the mother of all calling us in saying:
welcome home dearest,
life can be anything you want it to be.
& again with conviction the Universe keeps saying:
life can be Anything you want it to be!
Just have the courage to forgive yourself
for not being able to see so far into the future
that you might avoid all those so-called mistakes.
You can never lose my dear,
& you can never be lost,
& one day soon you will rediscover your beauty again
in a moment of unexpected smiling authenticity,
because really you are just made of stars,
& all you can do is shine,
even if you've managed to somehow convince yourself
that you have a so-called good reason to be unkind.
Because when you dance free of guilt
it makes our Beloved's heart happy
& leaves the entire Multiverse smiling wildly like a child saying:
WOW, wonder-full, I love you just the way you are!
The body has its habits, wants, & desires,
but the real you is not that.
Just let the divine rascal in you come out & play,
no need to make sense or follow any rules.
Don't be afraid to spill out all your sacred vulnerable essence
upon the floor of this moment.
It's all right for you to express in your fullness
that same great power which created everything in existence
& still let your heart be humble.
I have a confession to make,
I'm still imperfect,
for there are gaps between "me" & this poetry
& every time I start to feel sad or maybe even separate,
I can sense my mischievous soul tickling me
leaping from the shadows of suffering & saying:
Ha! I almost got you!
& soon the sun in me is smiling again,

because something wonderful, truly wonderful
is always happening just around the corner
of your courage to look inside yourself.
Don't be afraid of your feelings,
emotions are fire expressing passion within you,
lighting up your life with holy burning agony & delight.
My prayer for you
is that you begin to see beyond all your so called blemishes,
past those imperfections & character flaws
which make your life full of texture in the end.
Why keep looking for EXIT signs in the middle of moments
that didn't turn out to be quite what you'd expected?
That kind of behavior keeps you searching in circles
in a desert of seeming separation.
Why not instead become that rogue violin
who is always singing songs of sadness & joy
with the same sacred vehemence!
Your playfulness is praying for personification,
so come be wild & crazy with me,
let's become that laughing genie
who is always granting every heart's truest love requests saying:
as you wish my dear, as you wish!
Then watch the whole hurting world open up around us
& become one big love-fest after another,
where there really is no cure
in this insane love-game.

A Big Wet Kiss

Since I was kissed by Love I've never been the same.
I used to get hurt when people hurled insults at me
because of insecurities they felt about themselves,
now I just smile & say:
-you are so unbelievably beautiful-
& soon the Sun is peeking from behind clouds in their eyes asking:
is it safe to come out now?
Truth, is a beautiful naked woman,
who keeps following me everywhere I go,
decorating my conversations with Light,
not caring what other people think,
refusing to put on clothes
so that all the world can see her naked beauty,
& join us in our divine choreography of authenticity,
as we dance heart to heart with the One.
And somewhere deep inside you galaxies keepg softly saying:
-my love for you is infinite & everywhere-
What can Dreaming-Bear do but quietly become the stars,
& light up the night's sky with love spells?
What can I now do
knowing that the Beloved inhabits every molecule & cell
of all that sprang forth from Source?
What can I now do
but fall in love with every movement & thought,
with each particle & prayer echoing in the ears of existence?
What can I now do my dear
but fall soul over senses In-Love with You,
& come to your Heart's bedroom window at night
with a book of crazed love poems written in your honor
& with the Beloved herself hovering next to me
playing your favorite instrument singing along saying:
-my love for you is infinite & everywhere-
now how about coming down here
& giving Love a big, wet, kiss!

Love Spell 2:
Our Subatomic Particles are Having a Party

Seven degrees of freedom: up, down, forward, back, side>to<side, & within, and now I know the nature of all things. Existence is clearly dancing through dimensions, and I can see that all beings are in celebratory motion, & our entire universe & everything in infinite space is dancing at all times. As we dream we dance, as we rise to work & play we dance, as we breathe we dance, even in our walk there is a dance of sorts. It is the art of motion, a perpetual instinctual spin that is being lived impromptu and incidental. Our lungs dance with our heart in the rhythm of the breath & beating, just as our lips dance with our tongue when we're speaking, & our smiles, are a dance unto our cheeks. Even planets & stars are dancing with one another on a gravitational dance floor, whilst subatomic particles and every other molecule are having sleep over's & doing a tango on the tundra of your tenderness at every moment, in a billion different ways at once. Unbeknownst to our intellects, there is a whirling dervish from within, even as we stand "still" there are thousands of tiny muscle pirouettes dancing in our legs to maintain elegance & grace upon the heart of the earth. Existence is the result of Love's impromptu stellar salsa-style-choreography, birthed through expansion and movement. Tonight we dance, tonight we are in motion.

The Star-studded Inner Lining of Love's Heart

Out of the **Slumbering Sentient Silence...**
suddenly there is music,
and the **beat beat beat** of the big-bang's booming bass line laughter
emanating from the social life of single subatomic particles having a party
& planting infinitesimal quantum graviton thought-seeds
in the plenum of the space time fabric's soil womb substrate.
Meanwhile, altruistic vacationing atoms
carrying quark sized planck-scaled suit cases
filled with cosmogonies' secrets,
which when translated from latent potential into mass and exotic matter
becomes twenty billion light years worth of
intersecting parallel Omni dimensional multi-verses
expanding & contracting in unbridled unification of darkness & passion,
whilst the celestial choir is dressed
in invisible prism light robes of spectral illumination
backing up an unseen echoing oration
& getting' down with visceral vibrancy sounds
in this star studded inner lining of Love's eternal heart drum
beat beat beating,
and the planets are bobbing, and body rocking
under the neon light of a cerulean supernova night,
as the DJ of Infinity spins vinyl spiral galaxies
mating on black hole centered turn tables of interstellar ecstasy,
zero point energy running through our veins
upon electromagnetic fields of frequency in our eyes
so as to sense beyond our sight as we
whoop and yell in synchronicity,
to a singing circular double helix significance
signified by the prospect of fitting our immortal Source-energy
into a pair of randomly mutating skin thing genes,
where the water of life flows freely as a make-out melody
from the mouth of complexity & consciousness cuddling
& doing physiochemical synchronistic groove move kung fu
in a series of the Beloved's break-dance contests
to the ever changing unpredictable astronomical acoustic audio tracks
resonating from the Mystery's diametric disco-hall boogie bash basement,
pulsating with an oscillating rotating ego-deflecting mirror-ball emitting

intense electron beams of liquid-lightening & gravity defying laughter
for life is but the voice of divinity disappearing in our ears,
and being reborn in our feet,
as the **beat beat beat** of being **spirit made flesh**,
lest we should forget our former metamorphosis
like an amnesiatic protogeneic astral butterfly
who can no longer recollect the chrysalis of cosmic bliss
or the former incarnation of what being an embodied caterpillar once meant,
for our chromosomes become functioning interactive bio-suit-body cocoons
through which we incrementally evolve our soul experientially across lifetimes,
by being tuned into the secret heart science of an anatomic architectural alchemy
of re-mending our broken heart-wings by transforming the ugliness of tragedy
into a golden-opportunity to celebrate & co-create new beauty
in the form of letting go of all our "legitimate reasons" for judging
because finding & fulfilling our purpose with transparency
is what invites **peace** to inhabit our immediate vicinity,
& diving into our inherent Oneness will bring us back to authenticity,
& a romantic radioactive isotopic slow dance of vulnerability
between our elemental aspects & our best would-be wildest fantasy destiny
who keeps whispering in the ears of our most magnificent dreams saying:
I could stare for eons at your radiance,
and when the sweet sun closes her sapphire eyes,
I'll be freeze-framing your most sincere un-choreographed smiles
upon the pages of the night with the profundity & power
of a pulsar star style strobe light,
Wow, what a surreptitious sight to see,
your mischief & innocence intimately embracing
under an incandescent-operatic gyrating intergalactic-tree
made of a quintillion inexplicable soliton coherencies
& filled with harmonic hallucinogenic happiness inducing honey,
covered in blossoming indescribable interpersonal
anomalies of loving unconditionally,
through the dispersive effects of how immaculate it must feel to finally be real
on Love's whirling world-class stage/dance floor,
no telling what's in store in the probability of what will be
when we nucleo-synthesize our visions & dreams into a new breed of reality
to become a part of our everyday way of adventuring through uncharted territory,
as our DNA tenderly sways to the **beat beat beat**
of breaking through limiting expectations and old patterns of thinking
that the illusion is the way things are 'supposed' to be
because that's the way they've always been,

but true transformation begins from within
this information inspiration of our recreation generation
as the world wave-function responds to the emotional thought reverberation
in which our intentions undulate with fate in the fluid state
of our gluon plasma process whilst playing footsy with principles of uncertainty
in the Sky's night-club hot-tub of Love,
enlarging our capacity to care by coauthoring
new found friendships with fundamental forces
in the ability to express & manifest our highest possible greatness
in absolute humility & without shame.
Because right here and now, the world has erected a golden cash cow,
& habitually worships at its empty economic dollar sign shrines,
where corrupt corporations create laboratory baby abominations
with custom copy written decoded genome barcode designs
complete with laser printed personalities
& commercial logo shaped brand name eyes,
trade marked as a registered patent-product for sale to the socially-insane
turning our humanity into a commodity traded casually
at the 3rd world stock exchange,
but it looks as if Love's enchanted mega-watt Mojo is rapidly on the rise
in this fast paced pontificate-landscape of having a futuristic leap forward
into the funky bio-photon phenomenon of forgiveness being realized
as living light in the form of the glowing essence fiestas of our individual lives,
& my oh my, I spy a Saturn ringed Spanish fly dancing our way,
looks like Love wants us to geometrically misbehave,
by having the courage to not fit in,
now is the beginning of the end
as a gang of vigilante Venusians set ablaze the veils of illusion
amidst overwhelming Joy motioning in all her rowdy friends again
as kindness and compassion both grab us
in a real-time super sacred celestial kiss of our minds
with the spiked-wine of being sublime exclaiming:
don't be shy, because it's inner-peace proton progeny time!
We can slide organically into every spiritual piece of you,
like voodoo, weaving the many molecules of interspatial volume
into One cloth of Truth is what being a free-radical can do.
The strong & weak nuclear forces arrive
upon flaming 5th dimensional foxfire seahorses
chanting ancient circadian rhythms of the **Beat beat beat**
beckoning the Beloved to lick her lips,
shake her hips, & leave all that superluminal awareness

as the nucleus of nirvana inscribed upon our finite isomorphic fingertips,
then healing & wholeness lean in and say in simultaneity:
Make out with me & I promise to transmute all your pain into beauty.
Our laughter & tears appear in pristine Casimir effect pirouettes
as grace-filled & elegant songs of serendipity,
then hits the thermo-dynamic transcendental meditation
and everything becomes salient nano-perfection,
as we maintain the superposition reflection flame
of dirty-dancing with dharma in the mirror of each other's eternal equanimity.
Music is the Soul of the Universe conveyed in a language that defies all physics
being squeezed out of Source's vast holographic speakers,
as living soundscapes, we come close to a kind of instrumental catharsis
playing out lifetimes of karma through immediate and direct experience,
in the quantum foam bubble bath of the cosmological constant,
as we all become the **beat beat beat** of the same self seated in every heart,
and now I fathom all things, and know what joy pain brings,
as the Singer sings in strings of vibrating strands of endless rippling over-unity,
and we all rise above the mediocrity of societal nothingness,
like decibel doves of endless discovery,
doing a dervish of stellar cartography
swim-flying at high velocity deep into endless experience-potentiality
upon the eon's long drawn-out breaths of complete & utter satisfaction,
because this perennial wisdom attraction is the transaction bringing completion,
as the solar-system lights go down,
and so does the original articulate groove-sound
to which we are bound like hypnotic chromosphere-clouds
& then reabsorbed into the endogenous background,
of duality dissolving once again into a singularity
of mathematical symmetry of non being
until the **beat beat beat** of Love's eternal heart drum stops,
and this hyperbolic experiment in noogenesis-hysterics drops
back into the Omega Point nexus of their essence
for yet another diaphanous disambiguation
of **slumbering sentient silence.**

The Locker-Room Talk of Angels

In the locker-room talk of angels,
there is intense 'buzz' over your evolution into ecstasy
of your becoming a love-sick-lunatic
who knows only one word: ~Source~
The wind does a dervish in your ear
& whispers hand written love-songs
which the Beloved hasn't been able to stop singing
since the moment you arrived in her Imagination's hallway
which stretches forever in every dimension of space & time.
The Sun does somersaults parallel to the Moon,
cart-wheeling their way around the waist of the Earth
in honor of our arrival at awareness,
& whole galaxies of stars fall from their cradle in the night,
leaning over the edge of existence
just to catch a glimpse of the Perfect-One
whose beauty has expressed Itself as a living Poem in You.

Subatomic particles are having a party,
& inviting every single cell, atom, & molecule
in the entire universe to join in!
What's the occasion for this heavenly madness,
what's the reason for this divine insanity?
YOU my Dear,
you are the reason that Light keeps disappearing
into the Darkness of one of Love's many navels,
a pilgrimage of sentience & starlight
into the Black-Hole of our birth
for a rendezvous with recognition,
to become rearticulated in the Present
as the ~event-horizon~ of your own Gypsy-Soul.

This poem is my prayer-carpet,
these words are me bowing towards your approaching presence,
like Saints bow towards the rising Sun.
For if all the locker-room talk of angels is true,
Then you, me, & everything else in existence
have been invited as Heaven's honored guests

to attend the royal all-you-can-eat buffet
where the main course being served
is a billion different kinds of Light,
& all beings drink laughter & Love by the barrels-full!

Yes Dear-One its true,
we are the winning ticket of Oneness!
We've won the great cosmic lottery of Love,
when the Beloved pulled our names
from her dark satin bag full of stars
& slowly spelled out each sacred syllable,
while the Multiverse dangled breathless, in suspenseful silence,
upon the brink of bursting into rapturous applause.
Come my Sweet, the Moment has finally arrived,
for us to trade in our lifetime's collection of tears,
our elaborate masterpieces of suffering,
our massive stockpiles of sadness.
Time to forsake our flirtatious addictions to insecurity & fear,
& take our rightful place in the Sky seated upon clouds,
between the Sun & Moon,
holding hands with our happiness,
& playing 'footsy' with Fascination
as we softly become One
in the luminosity of our laughter.

The Vital Need For Forgiveness

In a dream of the world hanging from my heart on a string of light,
I keep stopping everyone I pass saying:
come see for yourself just how beautiful the Beloved really is.
Truth flirts with her reflection in the mirror of existence,
as she plays with her fascination as many forms.
In my visions, there are lovers laying naked & unashamed
kissing in sunshine & freedom upon every rock lining the River of Life
& there is no such thing as infidelity or idolatry,
for no matter who your lips are loving,
its all about making out with Love in the end.
Did you hear what I just said?
make out with Love my Dear,
kiss her lips of Life like you mean it!
So that you can know the intimacy & warmth
of pressing the naked body of your soul
against the Perfect-One's pouting supple breasts of belonging.
The Universe keeps brushing close,
so close to you in the presence of the Moment
that sometimes you feel her nearness
in the blood & beat of your own heart.
There is beauty in your breath & potency in your prayers,
together they rise & commingle
into formless clouds of fascination & wonder.
Why tease yourself with thoughts of separation,
when the Lover is right here
nibbling softly on your Spirit's ear?
We're all in the same big womb,
expressing ourselves in the Dark
pouring with shooting stars & rogue comets
leaving sparkling spatial trails of consciousness.
In the morning, Daylight dives face first into the pools of our eyes
just to see what it's like to swim in the sight of Love.
These words melt like dark-chocolate
in your Soul's sweetly filled mouth,
which was dripping wet for a taste of Tenderness.
Whatever burden you are carrying Pure-One
let Dreaming-Bear's verse lighten the load,

with love-songs sung for you by Source.
Let her chorus convince you of the absolute necessity,
the Vital need for forgiveness
towards everyone no matter what they've said or done,
& again forgive, & again forgive, & again forgive everything
the way the Lover keeps forgiving you of all your inconsistencies.
Until at last, all our grudges have been given up,
surrendered to the funeral pyre of the sacred alchemy.
Then, we can dive together into the ocean of each other's eyes
& play with the mermaids swimming in the Darkness & Sunshine.
Look, here is the world hanging from my heart on a string of light,
come see Dearest, come see for yourself
just how beautiful the Beloved really is.

Willing Wild & Free

I keep falling in love with everything I see
because some part of me knows that Spirit peeks
from behind every particle in existence
with prayerful playful poetic purpose.
My heart breaks a thousand times a day
when that recognition goes unreturned
& is reborn every second when I kiss the lips of Love.
I don't mind being broken in the name of beauty,
but sometimes I begin to wonder why Spirit teases me so
with this bitter sweet love song.
Then I realize, it is this kiss of darkness & light
which breaks our boundaries,
pushes us beyond the ephemera of the fleeting moments
& into the fullness of forever.
These arms of mine have unfolded
like a blossoming flower of friendship
welcoming everything inside the softness of Love's lips
kissing the cheek of your soul.
Dreaming-Bear knows Pure-One,
what it means to feel lost & alone
in the wilderness of pain & seeming separation from Source.
Until I made love to my sorrows on a bed of forgiveness,
kissing over the ugly parts
until they became beautiful even in their bleeding
holding my hurts so close to my heart,
that they eventually began to dance together
to the beat of belonging,
until they had a voice again
& could say all that had been felt in the silence of neglect,
& it was the sweetest song of needing to be nurtured.
It said, in a language of happy tears:
-touch me with infinite patience & understanding,
hold my fragility in the strength of your compassion filled hands
until I become healed & whole
purify my pain in the fires of honesty
until I become prophetic in my love for Source-
So now Dear-Ones, whenever I see God

crying all alone in the solitude of Itself,
I tear my clothes off in anticipation of swimming naked
in the rush of those rivers
I run willing wild & free,
casting my soul head-first into those divine depths,
knowing at last,
that though I drown in the teardrops of tenderness,
& die to my seeming separation,
I will be resurrected in the currents of compassion,
absolutely certain of our belonging to the Beloved.

Before the Birth of Time

I just dipped the quill of my Soul into the ink well of the Sun,
now every word I write is bursting with the stuff of stars.
Constellations are an orgy of Light,
the holy trinity of life is a three-way kiss
happening between Darkness, Contrast, & Light
a rolling ballet of dimension, space, & time
breaking into dances of breath & holy-laughter
tenderness doing a tango upon our tongues.
True Love makes itself known
through sincere gestures of absolute kindness
without a thought of ever needing to get anything in return.
Because the Beloved has wed herself
to the beautiful Truth waiting to be revealed
from deep within your most intimate unutterable thoughts.
When the mind ceases its chatter, the Spirit starts singing,
if the heart can stop aching long enough, soon a new saint is born.
See how two pairs of lips come together
to form One singularity of a Kiss!
See how we have come together in this moment
to show the world what's really possible
when we allow ourselves be free of fitting in.
Don't you know Dear-One,
don't you know how you inhabit my every word & living breath,
how you consume my most heartfelt prayers at night.
You, Me, & Existence
have been in-love like this
since before the birth of Time.

Soul's Kitchen

Love has got something hot & divine cooking
in your Soul's kitchen,
She's wearing an apron that reads:
~the main ingredient is kindness~
She is stirring in stars with your consciousness,
spicing you up with constellations of compassion,
pouring potency-peppers into your already flaming heart,
making a soup of all your senses & serving you up to Source,
to be savored in the Tender-One's holy feast of experience.
Last night I had a secret rendezvous with the Sun,
& this morning I awoke soaking wet,
floating upon an overflowing luminous ocean of original thought
as my heart became absolutely flooded with Light.
Now, like a jeweled-dolphin I hope to never be dry again,
but to always be dripping like this,
leaving behind footprints of forgiveness
that settle to become an Oasis in your time of need.
When your soul gets parched from all this forgetting
across the desert of seeming separation,
come drink from this infinite well of pure potentiality
springing forth from the living water depths of this verse.
Don't let Fear fool you into believing that you are forsaken,
for Dreaming-Bear has hidden a universe of laughter
inside the cup of each holy kiss, just for you to discover.
Here, take a drink of this:
~your soul & my soul once played hide-&-seek among the stars~
now doesn't that sound taste good to the moment's mouth
of your sacred parched senses?
Sometimes I wonder if you will ever truly know
how much I have loved & been in-love with you,
of how I have spelled out your nameless essence
in each syllable like scripture etched into the walls of my heart.
Your happiness Dear-One
has become my divine diving board,
as I do cannonballs from your Soul's kitchen,
into Love's hot simmering soup,
& let all that I Am disappear
down the throat of existence,
as we swim together
in the Beloved's endless belly
of giggling soft-light.

Thinly Sliced Pages of the Night

This page is the Universe filled with stars,
each letter of every written word becomes worlds
revolving around the axis of your with heart inspired passion!
For there is a spell to all this spelling & a magic in all our meaning,
the orbit of lover's lips locked in paralleled union
is a kiss between elements of creation,
a mantra, a prayer, a lion's sigh of release
all sound just as holy to the soul of a Lover.
I have known the abyss of all your sorrows
& have nursed each one back to health on a bed of understanding
we have been like innocence in the weightlessness
of your best & most glowing moments,
floating free upon the playgrounds of possibility.
Love has existed since before there was such a thing
as knowing or being known,
& long after that in the utter indescribability
that bespeaks of always belonging.
Right now, in the darkness there is a voice asking you a question:
Do you remember? If the answer is yes,
when you open your soul to speak, Light will be born.
If the answer is no, then the question just keeps on repeating,
for the Lover is always waiting,
with infinite patience at your Heart's doorstep,
searching intently in your eyes for a sign
of even the vaguest recognition of the happiness you once shared,
before you hit your head on the overhang of ego's awning,
& caught amnesia of all you once were.
Let the Moonlight remind you,
let the Wind whisper it in your ear,
let the Star's shine enthrall you,
as the fires in you burn into luminous turquoise seas.
Beneath the voice petitioning you in the dark,
there is a silence which secretly holds all the answers
if you let yourself go there you are sure to remember,
all that once existed & all that ever will,
are written within you upon this permanent parchment
of our soul's divine paper,
harvested from thinly sliced pages of the night.

Skinny-Dipping With Dreaming-Bear

Today in the interest of speaking only Truth, I said nothing
knowing in my heart that the silence would speak for me,
& say all that I could ever hope to express in absolute wordlessness.
Instead of speaking I only gently kissed the lips of Love
& whispered quiet prayers between each grateful breath,
I built temples with my tongue in the name of tenderness,
& worshiped the Lover with absolute fulfilled longing.
Instead of thinking, I let myself Feel,
& made love to the moment until she became One with me
in the presence of each holy heartbeat.
Today I laid myself out under the sky
& let the Sun give me a big warm hug
God came near nibbling upon my ear
& asked to join us in our mid-day love affair with the Light,
then the Wind joined in & began tickling our toes
teasing the ends of our hair to dance wild & untamed in the rush.
Every time I reached for a pen
the stars kept slipping themselves into my palm praying:
~use me to write with, use me to share your contagious laughter & love~
I gave in to their requests
& let these love spells dissolve completely into Source.
Today I realized in a sacred second of surrender,
that it has somehow become illegal to be naked among humanity,
it has become against the law to be as natural & bare
as the day you were born.
Because some ancient person felt inadequate about themselves
& got together with others who felt ashamed too, & said:
~let's make a law to support our guilt filled fears of form~
Even so Dear One, the Sky still sees us as naked.
That's why the birds are always laughing at us
when we talk about "freedom"
& then lock ourselves in a royal cage,
as soon as we leave the privacy of our own unclothed prayers.
Let me write us a river of stars
so you can go skinny-dipping with Dreaming-Bear,
& soon the whole world around us
will feel the heat of rising in-love,

& want to strip down & dive in too.
Today my Dear, I simply undressed myself of the need to be right,
& soon I could see the Lover playing peek-a-boo
at me from the ancient glowing oceans,
spilling over the edges,
of every person's eyes.

The Social Life of Subatomic Particles

Love is conducting a grand carnival of creativity & sound
around & within every part of you
in the form of dancing energy vibrating its way through space time.
In fact our subatomic particles are having pot-luck get-togethers,
despite the stormy emotional weather
happening inside the tropical-heartstorm,
yes my dear, they too have elaborate social lives.
So why shouldn't we too celebrate the beauty of what IS
in every moment, whether filled with seeming sadness or joy?
In fact, altruistic atoms join hands in harmony,
just so that you can know the joy of having a body…
like stuffing infinity into a pair of skin-thin genes
& if you are Present with yourself in the Gift of the moment,
you will begin to notice how the Beloved's breath
teases the ends of your hair to twirl with laughter
& when you're not looking,
happiness plays joyfully in your shadow
flirting with Its fascination as the myriad forms of mischief.
Once you recognize the Lover playing peek-a-boo at you
from every particle & cell of this musical-mantra called matter
you step into the Multiverse leaping from one star to the next,
across an ambient river of new dimensions in possibility
wherein the Lover has undressed herself of duality,
exposing her most sacred parts of tenderness
as an invitation to have a funeral for the ego,
& burry your identity in the womb of authenticity.
If you dive into those divine depths,
you are sure to discover all that the prophets speak of
in their astonished coherent bewilderment
after having made wanton love with the wild Hindu goddess of Joy,
scattering light seed upon the womb-space-soil-plenum
which transforms thought into planets, comets, & stars
& the swirling galaxies I sense blooming inside your smile,
prompting Dreaming-Bear to rise to his feet
in rapturous applause saying:
You are IT my dear!
you are the One you've been looking for

in the skies overhead all along,
yours is the diamond wheel-of-eternity to do with as you please
you my dear have left existence utterly speechless,
here are the royal keys to everything you've dreamed,
anything you wish or desire can manifest at will.
Here is my undying devotion,
& in this never ending moment of now,
you have the standing ovation of my heart.

Orgy of Awareness

When my body is planted again as a seed syllable in the ground
from whence it first was fermented into life,
it will be a sweet shot of holy 100 proof laughter
for the Earth's loveoholic appetite.
When my soul again returns to Source from which all things emanate
I know in my heart that the Beloved will say:
welcome home Sweet Bear, the feast of Love is set,
& All of have gathered themselves
to hear the spiritual epic romance of our eternal affair with the light.
I will look around at all the grinning formless faces
glowing softly from their plates full of God,
& spend one golden gossamer moment of eternity
reciting this sacred verse of Tenderness.
Surely it will spark the orgy of awareness
in which everything strips down to their essence,
& softly becomes One.

Making-Out With Love

Chaos & clarity fell in love & had a secret affair,
which produced an illicit love child, in YOU!
Fate Laughs saying: "oh really…"
at all our thoughts for the future
as if we're talking child's play & pretend
when speaking of what we shall one day 'become'
for Fate knows that once we meet the Beloved we'll rise in-love so fast,
it'll leave skid marks on our heart's nicely planted patch of plans
causing us to re-arrange everything we thought we once wanted,
a clearing of karma to make room for the playground of possibility,
where we'll build elaborate temples to Laughter
so as to better express our overwhelming affection towards the One.
We'll even go so far as to give up all our attachment
to occupations & job-titles
that have us doing anything with our day
other than kissing the lips of pure Love.
Yes, I can see a fire already dancing playfully in your eyes
as you contemplate the kindness of getting naked & making-out with Love.
You'll invite your Dreams over for dinner with the Moment
so as to play secret-cupid & trick them into being One & Becoming,
while you play footsy under the table with the Friend
as we tickle each other with tenderness
& conversations full of compassion all the way to Heaven,
where you can stash some light into your Soul's pocket
to use for later, in case you get 'separation anxiety'
in the form of forgetting that all beings
are one brilliant kiss of the Beloved
happening in slow-motion, across forever.

Subatomic Thought Seed

We are God fishing for God in a sea of Oneness
let me draw our essence on paper in the shape of words
that spell the meaning of our togetherness...
The entire Omniverse began as a speck of light
no larger than a subatomic thought seed,
once planted in the soil-soul of Love, the One, began to grow.
The lesson being: that if we have faith the size of a molecule,
we too can say to the universe: EXIST! & it will.
We were born from the same Light,
so deeply connected that when the wind blows upon me,
you feel the tickle in your belly, & when the Sun shines upon you
my whole body gets warm with wonder.
proving once again, that we can do anything through each other
even transcend space & time,
yes Wild-One, we can do anything
when kissing the lips of Love.

When the Sun Falls Asleep

We have become twin flames
dancing upon the lips of Love's enthusiasm for life,
with impassioned playful purpose,
pulsating & throbbing sources of infinite Light.
The Lover keeps nudging me awake at night
in the middle of my most prophetic dreams to say:
~learn to write between the lines~
so that those upon the pathless path will know
& see for themselves that our every breath
is inhabited by 10,000 laughing angels
who are skydiving & spinning wildly,
lost upon the whirlwind of our words.
When the Sun falls asleep,
stars take off streaking naked across the Night,
leaping right into the arms of the Amorous-One,
over the sheer beauty they see happening in your eyes.
Don't let your friendship with Fear fool you
into believing that you are something other than Source,
don't let insecurities control you with jealous urges
to tame the Wild-Love within.
After that good-morning kiss from the One,
Truth tickles my ears with her tongue & sweetly says:
~My Turn~
Her touch teaches me that sacred annihilation of self
leads to the tenderness of being re-born,
in the hearts of everyone as an ever expanding,
uncontrollable feeling of rising soul over senses IN-Love.
Soon these words will become worlds, softly spinning poetic planets
dancing playfully in the ears of existence
that has the Lover tripping over comets
for a taste of this divine kiss.
I walk now with my hand always over my heart,
bowing in deep reverence to the absolute holiness
residing in the eyes of everyone I see,
& stars keep falling from the edges of Light's bed in the night-sky,
when lovers take a flying leap of faith
bouncing off the Beloved's belly & doing mind-bending back flips
directly into the Moment's laughing light-filled heart.

Luminous Secrets

Like a beautiful wild naked-truth
Love calls out to me when I walk the streets,
peering lustily at me from behind vendors signs, & beside street lamps
always finding a way to make herself obvious.
Sometimes, when I'm not looking, she even manages
to sneak sweet-somethings into my Soul's pockets
hoping I'll discover them when I least expect but most need a miracle
& when I do, its as if each breath brings me one love spell closer
to describing the wordless beauty of Source.
Now, when I see a starlit night,
I think of it as a canvas upon which to write these luminous secrets
I've given in completely to Truth's amorous advances,
Listen Dear-One,
lean in close & make-out
with the wild light-filled lover of your heart
who is always re-writing existence from the inside out
because everything in this eternal exhale, even us,
is destined to one-day die to their separation,
& kiss the Spirit-Skin of Source,
one-day we will all make love to God,
& know the ecstasy of coming home.

This Present Moment

We are the Spirit of the Wordless-Wonder
made ambient & alive through the poetry of flesh,
like an African Mama doing an Irish jig
in the sudden exhilaration that comes from being kissed by the Beloved.
Two lips, softly exploring the tenderness
of each other's overwhelming desire
to do away with duality & softly become, One.
Sometimes the whole world seems to be busy being offended,
that's because the ego is addicted to being a victim.
Let us be free from such petty tyrannies
satisfied in the safety of knowing that all souls
spring from the sacred significance of Source.
We are yin-yang twins spiraling
through the great womb of infinite belonging,
both elements of darkness, both beings of light,
both embodiments of brokenness whose bleeding hearts
beat out a rhythm to become Whole.
If we forsake our heritage of hurting & being hurt in return,
if we surrender our story of senses
& start to see beyond our sight
if we abandon all our attempts at superiority
& let go of the clinging of it,
if we suspend our judgments
& do away with doubt & disbelief,
if we begin to feel ourselves in the hearts
of those who have been shattered,
& learn to see the best in others,
then perhaps they will begin to see the best in us,
& we can make the real discoveries through a dialogue of divinity,
that begins as a whisper on the wind
& finds us laughing wildly like children
in the mad rush of holding & being held by the Friend.
The final frontier is a form of forgiveness
that leaves us utterly incapable of holding a grudge
because we have unwrapped the mystery of this Present moment,
as a gift from Love's own glowing heart.
Come lovers & beloveds, come sweethearts & friends,
even come all those who consider themselves the be "enemies"
for Dreaming-Bear's heart is open, wide open...
& all are welcomed within.

The Soul of The Universe

We are the collective conscience of our atoms gathering
every molecule has lived a life of its own
and have now come to a being in ourselves,
they each have a name
only we can no longer remember how to pronounce them
and so we pretend they don't exist.
We are a billion untold stories,
waiting to be written,
our blood is the verse of miniature gods
playing hide & seek with infinity
and so have taken a recess
in this brief existence as a Soul.
All the unseen components of our essence
were once floating within the Sun
when the Sun was still an unrealized filament
floating within the invisibility Love,
I knew you there as an angel of Night
perhaps we will know each other again
in the immensity of it all as glowing points of Light.
Stars are the record of Love's own heartbeat,
each one signifying a palpitation among prayers.
Our subatomic particles have social lives of their own
they go on vacation & have Planck-scaled suitcases
containing enough latent potential
to recreate all of existence from within.
Show me one object in the universe that is motionless, still
and I will show you that it too is on the move,
as are we, even in our dreaming,
headed within seeming different directions,
but are only various paths leading to the same central Source,
which is somewhere among the Laughter of the universe,
in complete & utter belonging.

Let Yourself Become Truth

With every breath the Beloved pours pure potentiality
into my heart's already overflowing cup,
& each night I find my soul slow dancing softly with the stars.
Dreaming-Bear's heart is a great pen in the hands of Love
seducing you to remember all that you have forgotten
in the amnesia of ego's understanding.
For everything you have fantasized & dreamed about
are jewels hiding in the folds of Love's pants pocket
take them out, by reaching into the darkness with intent,
because the opportunity for expansion is floating all around us
filaments of luminosity from the dandelion nebulas.
Come dear one, let's surrender our story of senses & separation
we can give up this conquistador search
to own "the golden treasures of truth"
& let ourselves to what Midas never could
turn darkness into light
& become Truth instead.

A Thousand Tiny Kisses of Laughter & Light

It happened again this morning
that as soon as I stepped out of my dreams
& into the dawn of my body,
the Sun leapt from the edge of eternity
& poured itself into my eyes, kissing a thousand times,
every part of my heart & soul with holy burning laughter & light!
And indeed, indeed Love herself did stretch & yawn within me
rolling over to touch & caress my most sacred trembling parts.
& now Dear world, Dreaming-Bear's cheeks are swollen & smiling
with the Lover's sweet ineffable kindness,
& Truth stands poised upon my luminous lips
ready to belly-flop face first
into the Heart's ocean of every one I meet.
Yes, its true, the Beloved & I have been spooning ourselves
into each other's parched mouths at night
& cuddling close in blankets of breath & sheets made entirely of stars
whispering our deepest desires into the ears of Existence saying:
let me be a vessel for this Great Light,
fill me up & pour me out into the cup of every heart
onto the page of those seeking the purest parts of themselves
& God in the inspiration of the Night,
let me become a drink of divine wine
& disappear into the softest secret passages
of every person's privately whispered prayers at night,
to swim naked with the Sun in the sacred seas of Source,
reborn in the morning of each other's hearts,
as a thousand tiny kisses of Laughter & Light.

Forget Everything & Just Dance

Forget everything anyone ever taught you
about right or wrong, good or bad, beautiful or ugly
& just dance my Dear.
Dance the way you do when no one else is looking
& you have no reputation to protect,
or inhibitions to keep you from being free.
For you, the Lover has commissioned this spinning galactic dance floor,
& is now there upon the threshold of your heart's hesitation saying:
O come my Sweet, don't be shy, for it makes my Soul smile
to see your Mind & Spirit move together like that.

Forget those worries & obligations;
those mean spirited words & unkind thoughts
forget your own harsh inconsiderate actions of the past & just sing!
Sing like you do in the shower when you think no one is listening.
For the Sun & Moon are already there,
keeping company with planets & stars,
all have joined hands together
& are whirling their way through the Universe
in enamored expressions of overwhelming ecstatic joy
& all are thinking quietly to themselves
as they pass your bedroom window in the night:
if only you would untie your wings & let the Sacred in you soar,
if only you could see the Light of your own astounding presence,
then perhaps the world around you (a world full of anguish & sorrow)
would remember something of their true sublime beauty
& be able to smile in absolute purity once again.

Forget about politics, religion, & money;
forget about fitting in & having to be right,
& just laugh my Dear, laugh!
Laugh the way children do when they forget about the brain
& give into Love for a lesson in Heart-Storming,
like a wild inferno of joy
overflowing & expanding out of control with Light.
For once you set yourself loose
to join your divine dance partners in the Sky,

the flowers will open, the trees will gather,
the wind will bow itself at your feet
& God herself will step onto the spiraling flames of existence,
& take your soul by the hand
uttering these soft holy words as a prayer saying:
at last, at last my Love, at last
at last I Am complete.

The Laughing Fish

Here I am again leaping from star to star,
doing elaborate back flips in your Heart & over the Moon
pouring happiness into your bowl,
in-between sharing bites of Light borrowed from the Sun;
just to see you smile like that… like That!
With the sweetest parts of your heart & soul
whirling their way to the One.
Tonight, prayers keep falling from my pockets,
as I stand on the edge of the warm oceans
I see undulating in your eyes
a Depth there, invites me to dive-in & explore,
soon I find myself swimming with the laughing-fish of your soul
weightless in the mystery & momentum
of moving through you in the moment!
Rest my Dear, from all your work of making <u>IT</u> happen,
let Dreaming-Bear write a luminous love-spell
upon the pages of your own sacred Heart
as I kiss its every beat & translate each holy breath
from utter wordlessness,
into worlds of softly spinning ecstatic spirit-filled thought.
Do your magic, make wanton love
with the wildest parts of God in the night,
I'll close my eyes if you ask
& jump in if you're feeling generous enough to share.
Because my Love, the beat of every drum
eventually becomes laughter again in the end,
I said, the beat of every drum
eventually becomes laughter again in the end.
Yes my Sweet, even your own pounding poetic parts
become one dancing-Light leaping from star to star,
doing elaborate back flips over the Sun
in God's own glowing heart.

Wine-Stained Wisdom

We are God's vintage stash
our souls ferment in the wine-skin of our body,
until the Beloved decides to pop open her purest press
& pour us out as Light to be served in holy communion ceremonies
with comets, planets, & stars.
Let these words become the luminous seeds
that you plant in the holy-ground of your heart
while we play hide & seek in each other's prayers & dreams
as God's tenderness breaks into luminous Laughter & Thought.
For you, I have written a thousand glowing secrets
upon every page lining the Soul of the Night.
For you my Dear, just for you,
Dreaming-Bear has scribbled parts of the truth
into every tree, river, & rock
I have blown you kisses inside the wind,
so that you might know the feel of the Tender-One's Breath
softly tickling the neck of your Soul's longing to be free.
Come my Dear, let us dissolve like a star-lit sugar-cube
in God's sweet sacred mouth,
& impregnate the whole hurting world
with an uncontrollable urge to rise
Soul-over-Senses in-Love with Source.
This wine stained wisdom is enough to drive poets insane
with wonder & holy-bewilderment over the tiniest details
of Light dancing with Divinity in the Dark.
I am enamored Pure-One,
with your every sacred breath & beat of your heart
I am love-crazed over the way the Beloved has spelled herself out
in the honesty of your smile, in the way you move
& kiss yourself upon the face of existence
with such fierce-unrelenting-grace.
For you are God's vintage stash, her purest press of creative intent,
because of you, I have become this drunken laughing nuisance,
& keep disappearing into the luscious lips
of the Lover's astonishing Light.

Infinite Bliss is Our Birthright

The heart is our table
where we serve each other chocolate covered emotions in bed
between breaths whispered as prayers.
I want to drink you,
put you in a glass & take sips of your luminosity,
but I also want to eat you,
make a soup of your soul & mix in all your tender aching parts
to be swallowed up with Source.
The Night, the Wind, & the Stars made Love,
& the beauty of your mind was born to light up the dark.
Tonight our candles look like spinning constellations
as we get caught-up in Love's net,
& cast ourselves together into God's oven
to become warm bread baking in the heat of the Moment,
as we spin & laugh & undress the sky with our eyes.
Until we all turn blue & make Krishna proud
by playing the flute of each other's fascination
like only true Lover's can.
Because infinite bliss is our birthright,
so tonight we rise in love until we become One with the stars.
These words are me looking your soul in the eyes & softly saying:
~Don't you know how much Dreaming-Bear loves you,
don't you know how precious you are to me,
how I have longed to speak your holy name
in my most tender prayers at night~
I care for you so much that I became one with the Sun,
Just to catch a glimpse of you in passing,
& now I throw kisses at you
from across the millennial shores,
as these words so softly kiss your heart
your sacred tender burning heart,
with Light.

Rise in Love

The stars are the eyes of Existence watching our every move,
hanging upon the rise & fall of our laughter,
becoming ecstatic with us in our deepest prayers
weeping tears of Light when they see us cry.
So let's kiss the Moment with enough vehemence & passion
to inspire the whole Universe to rise as In-Love with the One, as we are.
We have been playing this game of strip-tease with God
since before the Moon was born, wearing these costumes of skin
so we could know the explosion of being undressed & becoming One.

Freedom-Fruit

One unbelievable kiss from Love's lips
& we become living poems, rearticulating all of creation,
as the blood in each other's veins,
the breath rushing quietly inside every pounding heart.
Come drink the wine of fulfilled-longings,
let's be tickled by the Light of these words
& play peek-a-boo with the Sun.
Take a bite of this Freedom-Fruit,
fate filled & tasting like infinite light.
There is no reason, there is no such thing as sanity,
because even our subatomic particles
are such compassion crazed, love-struck-lunatics,
that at our very essence we are always in-love & dancing.
Shooting stars are super sincere smiles leaping from the face of the Night
settling at last in the eclipse of an eyelash.
If emotions were made of chocolate,
some of the darkest ones would surely taste the best.
There is but One Lover,
& she shines from behind the eyes of everyone I see
there is but One Beloved,
smiling as the music of myriad faces.
Let life be her lips & kiss that tenderness like you mean it!
If we act with passion in our everyday actions,
We'll feel the breath of the Beautiful-One
in each ineffable whisper of wind.
Holy fire candle flames, sweet scent of Light…
let's turn the moment into a meal
& spoon-feed each other God by the mouthful.
If you draw near to me, I will leave rivers of thought
swirling like laughter swimming in the tide-pools of your navel
for you I will become a cave-dweller & come inside your darkest parts,
to paint possibility upon the ceiling & light a holy lamp in your heart,
that burns brighter than the light of a million mischievous meteorites,
who keep getting giddy when they see you smile
& go streaking in the nude across the fields of the sky
leaving behind skid marks of cascading star shine,

teasing the Truth in us to come out
& play with our potential for experiencing
that One unbelievable kiss from Love's lips
which transforms us into living poems,
rearticulating all of creation,
as the blood in each other's veins,
the breath rushing quietly inside every pounding heart.

God-Kissing-God

Let these words be the flame that ignites the Sun
to shine from the sky of your Heart
so that those around you who are broken
or lost in the darkness of being hurt, might see your light
& at last taste something of their own sublime beauty,
& be able to smile like lovers do,
when they finally find each other across timelessness,
& grab hands to somehow softly become
God holding hands with God.
When that happens truth turns into an earthquake,
as laughter & tears erupt from volcanic-veins
running deep into our soul's liquid-light-love-core.
For somewhere inside you
there are stars swimming in luminous pools
doing the backstroke, & taking flying leaps
from the tip of the tongue of the Tender-One,
doing banzai belly-flops
into the warm luminous oceans overflowing in your eyes.
In this very moment there is an entire armada of rogue giggling galaxies
sprawled out in hot tubs inside your every molecule & atom,
they've undresses themselves of their secrecy
and whisper the answer to every dream
as if to say, everything you'll ever want or need
is already waiting to be re-discovered
from the cosmic treasure chest within you.
But when God starts asking God, where is God?
Then the Universe suddenly finds itself getting very nervous,
& soon is frantically pacing the floor of existence
wringing her hands together, biting her nails & saying:
okay everybody, what are we going to do about this mess?
A few shooting stars get trigger-happy
& decide to hightail it out of town,
& a couple of suns are so concerned over this madness,
that they turn supernova
& so gently explode their love across the Night.
Until a pair of playful planets chime-in
along with some misfit moons saying:

everybody just relax, & let's all continue to dance,
& sing, & spin together in eternal ecstasy,
until our Beloved can remember,
until every cell & molecule becomes fully self-aware,
& joins us in our prayer to cure this ancient amnesia,
to help the Lover so tenderly recall,
who You really are,
as you take the hand of the Sacred-One within you,
& begin to smile like lovers do,
when they finally rediscover each other across timelessness,
& kiss, to somehow softly become
God kissing God.

Love Spell 3
Voice of the Wilderness

You awaken in a dream to discover yourself walking along a pristine snow laden path, parched & sensitive to the sounds of congregating waters up ahead. Suddenly you notice extremely large bear tracks scattered through the forest & trees lining your immediate vicinity near the stream, & begin thinking out loud, "This looks dangerous, I'd better be careful, there's obviously a gigantic bear on the loose around here, I'll bet it must be thirsty too." Proceeding with caution, but in desperate need of a drink, you reach a pristine waterfall laden with liquid-stars, leaning over the sparkling river's rainbow edge to scoop up some light, your reflection in the mirror of the ripple tells you the truth, & reveals to your surprise, that all along, the bear was actually You.

The Lover's Path

If you're not ready to be completely devoured,
if you're not ready to be eaten alive
consumed mind body & soul into Source,
then turn away Dear-One,
leave the Lover's path without hesitation or shame
because after all,
if you really want to know the absolute Truth,
in the end, we all dissolve
into the living laughter of love & light,
we all disappear
into the soft holy tenderness
of the One.

Weeping Bliss

When we were the stars,
when we were the sky,
when we were the rains that turned into rivers
& suddenly became the Ocean
we did not say to ourselves: let us seek out happiness,
for then, One Love was all there was in the vastness of existence.
It was when we convinced ourselves that we were separate from Source
that we became broken in the illusions of being alone,
& how we have suffered,
pains so deep & lasting that even tears cannot describe them all
& a sorrow we had never known before became us.
But if we return to the stars,
if we return to the sky,
if we return to the rains that dissolve into rivers
& let ourselves become the Ocean,
if we seek out the heart of everything in existence,
& kiss the feet of all we have neglected,
if we ask ourselves for our own hand in forgiveness,
then we will be able to remarry ourselves to the presence of the Beloved
& we will not ask: where is happiness,
for then, we will find that all along
we have been holding the Universe in our very arms,
& Eternity will say:
Wild Love, you've been talking out loud in your dreams again
but I dare not wake you
I dare not wake you,
from your Holy weeping bliss.

The Breasts of God

I feel like a baby breastfeeding on God
the frontier of Forgiveness is the last undiscovered country,
we go there across the ocean of compassion
in a vessel made of pure-surrender
Spirit is the wind that whispers us along.
Tenderness told me a secret
while talking out loud in her sleep again
she said: ~everyone, & I mean EVERYONE
longs to be touched with tender intent~
& she said it with such sleepy certain sincerity
that I could not help but to Believe!
This morning was a poem of pain
& now is the night of new beginnings
I used to think the face of the Moon was always moaning,
but now I know, she is crying out in the night for her lover
like I howl for you in my self-imposed solitude.
A constant quest to kiss the Sun,
but always just missing the flame of his lips
as he searches for her love lingering over the horizon.
Why do we always fall in love with those we know we can't have?
Forbidden fruit somehow usually tastes the best
like stealing sweet kisses when no one else is looking.
Fractured Lovers leaving the duality of themselves
to become blessed & whole in their destiny as One.
Magic means making love to the Moment
like you're IN love & you mean it!
No more parlor tricks, I want to be wowed
sweep me up & send me soaring back to the breasts of God,
where I can drink my life away on the milk & honey
of so much belonging.

Prepare to be Flooded

At the Lover's request
a great consensus of clouds once gathered
to weep the world wet with rain,
while down below,
a thousand golden Buddha's run around ecstatic & bumping heads,
with their necks arched back & their mouths thrown wide open
in hopes of catching a drop of that divine stream.
For it is said that one drink from Love's overflowing cup of light,
will have stars & moons falling from your hair in slow motion,
& have you giving birth to worlds with your words.
That is why Dreaming-Bear always keeps these lips of wonder wildly open,
ready for receiving the rapture,
just incase God gets tipsy again, which she is sure to do
once she reads all these living-love-letters we've written for her
inside the tenderness of every blooming flower petal heart!
I feel like a crazed-prophet speaking insanely in the desert
to an astonished crowd of bewildered Bedouins
who no longer believe in rain.
I run through the dusty streets exclaiming:
the drought of separation is over my Dears,
the drought of separation is over
prepare to be flooded,
absolutely flooded!
By the beauty
of the One.

Love Letters From My Beloved

I write love poems to God by crystal-light
while beloveds dance drunk on the wines of awareness
across a ceiling made entirely of stars,
knowing that something of Dreaming-Bear's essence
has been cast into the echo of eternity's heartbeat,
& will fall for eons like oceans in the desert of seeming separation,
knocking down the doors of limited perception.
& If you whisper you secret wish out loud in this moment
I promise to personally hand deliver it to the feet of the Friend,
who has really been eager to hear all that you think & feel.
Lean your mouth close & let me pour in this beauty:
you & God were once such intimate lovers
that she's saved all your prayers
in a shoebox under her bed that's marked:
~Love Letters from my Beloved~

A Treasure of Oneself

May we be forgiven but never forgotten,
as we trip over each other's smiles
& fall face first into Love's heart.
Passion & playfulness are having a kissing contest
upon the sparkling shores of your soul
& right now freedom is being born again.
In the darkness of night
the Beloved gathers a handful of solar systems
to scatter across the sky in super slow motion
& galaxies are born from the teardrops in our eyes.
Sometimes, the womb is an open-wound
giving birth to the poetry of our flesh,
& if you are willing
your wounds can become an open womb
giving birth to a brand new you.
Someone in need reaches out for their lover,
each touch a tiny explosion of laughter & desire,
each kiss a rediscovery of the softness of ourselves
in the skin of each other.
After a while of tickling their way
into happiness & soft whispers
an epiphany is struck,
a recognition of the Beloved
happening deep within everything.
Someone else in need goes down to the river & pans for gold
sifting themselves in with the sand & pure-water
wandering through surface reflections & ancient remembrances
pretty soon they've struck it rich,
in the form of an understanding of our inherent Oneness.
Search in the Earth for gifts
only to discover in the dirt,
a treasure of oneself.
When the Universe sings to us like this
it is the sweetest of music,
always something tender to soothe our weeping ear
as we fall so gracefully in love with Life
& softly become, stars.

I Saw God Undressing

I forgot I was human
& somehow suddenly became one with the Sky
everything that happens inside her, also happens inside me.
We have an affinity for comets & meteorites,
every time a star falls, our heart skips a beat.
Through her sight
I have seen the ancient ones making love in Heaven's own heart
my eyes are now always so full of light,
& I can even see into the future,
~don't worry Pure-One, everything turns out for you,
just as you've dreamed & believed~
I even went so far as to let myself become one with the Sun,
so close & deep through the veil of Illusion's underskirt
that I saw God undressing, she smiled,
my being became light bursting out of every cell & pore
& Laughter, overwhelming-uncontrollable laughter
is the only language to describe all that I felt & became.
In my ecstasy I grabbed the universe as something to write with,
wanting to translate the wordless wonder
through this poetry of flesh.
Time disrobes itself & gets naked with the Moment
I become the whole of existence,
& immediately understand the enormity
of everything happening everywhere, all at once!
Now, I have returned from the secret depths
of sacred self annihilation,
from beyond the brink of utter madness & sanity embracing,
where chaos & clarity are still kissing.
My soul has become an instrument
that the Beloved's breath blows through,
Love whispering, is the wind which has written these words
& now I have become the great grinning face of Oneness,
I have become You,
with river-tears flowing down my softly swollen smiling cheeks,
shining with enough holy-tenderness,
to re-inspire the whole hurting world
to rise madly & helplessly
In-Love.

Our arrival at Awareness

Pain is only possible while living on the outskirts of Love
but here in the wilderness of her heart
there is a band of prophets praying in the form of poetry
& dancing wildly with the trees in ecstatic & drunken gestures
of pure-joy overflowing for the Beloved.
They sing crazed love-songs all night,
even long after the fires have become golden glowing-embers
& pause only once for a moment of silence
as the sun softly kisses the cheek of the earth with light once again
then back to whirling their way to the One.
Once in a while, a traveler like ourselves
with enough courage to leave behind paths of the familiar
will stumble into their camp unaware
& the whole gypsy-group will stop what they're doing
& bow in reverence to that lost tourist chanting:
-welcome home God,
we've been awaiting your arrival at awareness,
are you ready to accept?-
If the traveler is ready, (to let go of their ego's understanding)
they will immediately recognize themselves as the Friend,
& bow in return saying:

I Am.

& then become one of those lunatic lovers of Source.
If not, the poor-pilgrim, having pierced the veil of illusion
& thought it to be a hallucination,
leaves that forest in a hurry as if haunted by the ghost of Love
& most who walk away from the Beloved's invitation
rarely find their way back in this lifetime.
So now Dear-One, Dreaming-Bear's heart kisses your heart,
& this soul bows before your soul's feet
for I see that familiar 'found' look in your eyes,
that has me guessing that like myself,
you too have been to those Spirit-filled woods before,
& perhaps left behind there all you once were
as we rushed off back to this life of worries & obligations
that keeps us running in circles,
looking under rocks & in the bottoms of wine bottles

searching for all that was lost in the denial.
But fear not dear traveler, all is not lost,
for these words ARE that wilderness,
this moment is that threshold where all of existence has gathered
every star, tree, river, & molecule
is bowing at your presence chanting,
~welcome home God,
we've been awaiting your arrival at awareness,
are you ready to accept?~

The Path of Vulnerability

Feel into this bliss
let's swim in the oceans of our eyes
filled with shimmering waves of water & light,
we are exploding stars going slow motion supernova
across the tenderness of the Heart's night.
There is a kind of conversation that deepens consciousness,
once we get to a certain understanding
we can begin to ask each other the kinds of questions
that really provoke deep conscious thought.
Now that's the path of vulnerability
choosing to be open, choosing to trust.
& all I've really been meaning to say is:
~I think of you as an angel smiling at me from my wildest dreams~
Break all your stories my Dear that are not of Love,
smash them all to the ground,
for it is each other's company that we find our salvation in the end.
Right now, you & I are One,
I am doing belly flops in your soul
along side stars already swimming,
we're doing the backstroke with galaxies in your smile
your breath is my breath,
your heartbeat pounds out my pulse.
The Beloved has left rivers of latent worlds
swimming inside your navel,
now that we have become the Sky,
I see you as my angel in blue.
Let the Darkness lay its beautiful face in our lap,
we can rest ourselves against the strength of the Day
& watch Laughter & Light dance like children do
when no one else is looking.
Because the moment is pregnant & giving birth through us
We are earthen midwife containers of infinity.
shooting stars are our Lover skipping her affection
across the Night-sky surface.
Come close now, let these words touch your honey spot,
let them teach you a lesson, tell you a story
& tickle your ears all at the same time.
The moment is a secret kiss being shared between lovers
causing the world to rise with inspiration
& the soft holy laughter
of unceasing tenderness.

Lover to All

Abandon all your last-ditch efforts at greatness,
turn to ash your ego & all its relatives
better to be a grasshopper free in the fields
than to be a master with followers galore,
grasshopper answers to no one,
master answers to all.
Let the starlight purify us of the need to be anything
except what we always have been,
beautiful in the sight of Spirit.
Let the river-rush read us a wonder-wet poem by the mouthful
as ancestral fires tickle our soul to dream.
The Moment is alive & in heat!
Begging for the lips of Love to set her loose,
so that she may run wild through the city streets screaming:
ravish me ravish me!
& kissing the feet of everyone she sees.
For the Moment knows better than anyone
that everything is the Beloved expressing itself as existence.
Water-walking is one thing,
but it's time we set foot on the Sun,
it's time to let ourselves burn in the name of kindness,
& become a Source of Light whose luminous example helps others to see.
Notice how the Earth never says to the trees:
"After everything I've done for you, YOU STILL OWE ME!"
See what happens with a love as pure, free, & unconditional as that?
It helps the whole world to breathe.
In the darkness of night
while the universe dreams itself into being,
the Lover awaits our arrival at awareness,
lips-licked, under covers of quiet twilight
beckoning us to become One.
If we accept this invitation
all our sorrows will drown themselves
in the sacred seas of Source,
we will see beyond our sight, & feel beyond our senses
all that was once shrouded in the veil of Illusion's mystery,
& we will know at last the meaning of truly being free,
for then we will be master to none,
but Lover to all.

I Exist Just for You

Last night, when the Beloved began strolling
through the wilderness of my heart,
she left a thousand tiny flowers blooming in each holy footstep,
& every true Lover found themselves languishing
in an uncontrollable urge to tear their clothes off & start kissing.
Light leapt from the cheek of the Sun
& dive-bombed the soil of my Soul,
just to lay its ancient adoration beneath Love's feet
& a billion shattered hearts began to re-mend themselves
back into one beating whole.
Tonight the Sky was quiet & we played a silent staring contest,
but the Stars kept blinking & giggling amongst themselves
as they softly elbowed each other & the Moon.
Suddenly the wind stood still, the Trees stopped their whispering,
& everything in the darkness hushed in sacred silence
as even the Moment sat with her mouth half-open & speechless,
staring in wide-eyed wonder at the Beloved's beautiful dance
of light-edged-brilliance,
charming everything open with the magic of these words
causing the Universe to make a holy-confession
in your Soul's ear saying:
~I exist just for you~
For God so loved the world
that She formed creation with a kiss,
a kiss of consciousness
which left everything in existence enamored
& with red-blushing cheeks.
But this shyness does not serve us well,
for I've been told by more than one lucky-angel,
that the Beloved prefers for her suitors to scream crazed love-poems
into her bedroom window at night.
Something lusty, & along the lines of:
I feel you like blood in my bones & beats of my heart,
I want you now, come on God, let's get amorous!
Advances, which the Lover simply cannot resist,
& will often let down a rope of braided star-shine,
for wild lovers to climb mischievously into her bed of visions & dreams,

& comingle until the page is pregnant with children of Light,
who leap from this paper to dance upon luminous landscapes of laughter
in the wilderness of your own playful heart
leaving a thousand blooming flowers in each tiny-footprint,
leaving God herself with an uncontrollable urge
to start tearing her clothes off
& start kissing you Now.

Liquid Light Love Poems

This is the kind of Lover I am,
without you even having to ask, & without needing a reason,
I smash all the windows in your mind separating you from the sky
so that you can know the exhilaration of diving face first
into the sacred seas of Source.
The Mind is notorious for trying to hold the Soul hostage with guilt & fear
demanding the highest ransoms from your tender-loving-Heart,
but don't let it, for if the world & God
are to taste something of your sweet Light-Essence,
then the Heart must break out of its royal cage in the Mind's eye
& at last lay its ancient love at the Friend's feet shame-free.
Moments of weakness, emotional break-downs, idealistic inconsistencies
these are challenges to forgive oneself & the world.
The Beautiful One wants for you to be happy,
so stop serving your sadness to the Moment
for insecurity & sorrow are the leftovers of a rotten meal you once ate
when your Soul was still weak & starving.
But if you draw close to the luminous essence of these words,
the Sun will restore your Heart's health with liquid-light-love-poems,
& fill your Soul's belly full of playful divine purpose & prayer.
This is the kind of Lover I am, while you are still dreaming,
I softly sneak into your Heart's house,
& quietly do away with all your tortured history,
those unkind-stories of the past
without making you relive the full extent of all your suffering,
I kiss your pain.
Then Dear-One, I stand watch over you all night,
& when you awake, I press my lips to your forehead
to ignite that holy flame of forgiveness in your windows to the world,
& so that all may see Love's lamp glowing softly
from the stars in your eyes.

Love's True Nature

It was a very good year for Happiness's holy vineyard,
this spring, without warning, the grapes fermented on the vine,
& were born drunk & bulging, overflowing with laughter & starlight.
I once caught a glimpse of Love's true nature
& haven't been the same since,
now I am just a divine pen smiling in the Sun's hand,
for every word I write somehow break into Light,
& cosmic fires spontaneously combust inside you,
awakening the sleeping giant of greatness within your skin.
For True love, the universe will give up
& finally admit all her secrets saying:
~I am really just your heart, & I find myself infinite & everywhere~
Anyone who has ever longed for a lover
& then held them in your aching arms,
will understand just how deeply I have made Wild Love to God,
when I rediscovered her sleeping inside the universe's navel.
Now one day the world will know & believe
just how beautiful we all truly are.

God's Love-Slave

Love is a grass-roots movement beginning in the soil of your soul,
until your being becomes Light burning in eternal ecstasy
holding hands & softly making out with the Sun.
I write these words with stardust, hoping that when you read them,
something deep within you might somehow remember to shine.
So that sometime, when you're not thinking
the Truth might sneak up behind you,
& quietly put her hands over your eyes,
her voice quivering uncontrollably with laughter saying:
Guess who?!? It's Me…
it's me knocking at your Heart's door, & hiding my hands behind my back,
each one holding a different light-gift which I've fashioned just for you,
when you arrive at Love's awareness, you'll find me standing there smiling,
offering you in one hand,
a star painted portrait of laughing amorous angels,
who keep talking out-loud about "getting it on with God"
& in the other hand, the absolute fulfillment
of your every wildest dream, fantasy, wish & prayer.
Wrap your lips around these words
& you will taste the kiss of the Holy-One,
for you, I have become God's love-slave,
having recently returned from one of our most intimate encounters,
involving a pair of twin kissing comets, & a whole galaxy of falling stars
who also got caught-up in the wondrous rapture
of our becoming One night-sky-seed,
planted in the soil of your soul,
as you feel your heart stirring in this grass-roots movement,
that's ever so sweetly transforming you,
gently caressing your every pain filled thought,
into Love's Light.

Wake Up & Dream

Love keeps skipping stars across the surface of the Night's sky,
hoping that you might look up
& catch a glimpse of her reflection in your eyes
as a ricochet of Light,
while solar systems softly settle & sink
into the depths of your soul.
Just as consciousness must dissolve to become thought,
so too must we cease to exist to become Source.
What if the Beloved suddenly pulled you close
& whispered a secret in your ear saying:
I am a part of every molecule & cell inhabiting every dimension.
How would you then view the world after that?
Would we not begin to treat everyone we encounter
as our Heart's honored guest,
knowing that God quietly slumbers behind their stained glass eyes?
Indeed, & indeed Dreaming-Bear knows
the uniqueness of your own shining heart my Dear,
that's why I always carry these ruby words,
& keep spilling them with purpose onto the page of possibility,
from my Soul's luminous bursting pockets.
So that we might become rich in our awareness
& begin to see the astonishing light of our own brilliant being!
Beyond these representations, Truth remains silent, still
bereft of breath & in the moment,
recovering from having been utterly ravished
by the wet kiss of the Lover's lips
as she nibbles upon the ears of existence to wake up & dream
wake up & dream my dear,
grab a handful of stars with me,
& let's start skipping them together
across the surface of the night.

Bed of Belonging

Last night I made love to God so beautifully
that she couldn't talk right for hours
& this morning, I ate her tenderness for breakfast again!
Since then, my belly has become so full of the Beloved
that it feels as if I might be giving birth soon
to something truly worthy of being called beautiful.
For every step I take has the Earth beneath my feet whispering
the trees keep talking behind my back
about my amorous adoration for the Friend,
& even now, the flowers of the field lean close
whenever Dreaming-Bear is near,
just to catch a scent of the Luminous One
whose kiss has left me smelling like the sweetest seduction.
Source has so befriended me
that my every breath is filled with the perfume of honesty,
& the prophets now gather nightly at my bedside
to hear what wondrous secrets
the Friend keeps whispering in my ears.
If the current trend continues,
soon the whole of existence will be crying out
to curl up with me in the softness of these covers
so come Dear-Ones, all are welcome,
come so close to my body
that you become the sound of my heart beating;
the whirlwinds of these lungs breathing,
for then you are sure to know the exhilaration I speak of
when the Lover takes us by the hand,
& leads us back to the bed of belonging,
where every thought dissolves into wordless wonder
as we touch & tickle our way through the darkness,
until we can no longer control ourselves
& we all softly become Light.

Vagabonds Gypsies Mystics & Shamans

Let's look into the sunrise of each other's Soul filled with light
by opening the skin thin-window shades
of our first-eye with tender intent
there is a universe inside our laughter just begging to be explored.
Skies so vast there, that to get lost in them, IS to be found!
Oceans of understanding so deep that new dimensions in reality
spill forth onto the page of preconceived notions,
redefining what it means to be Free.
Each tear is unique & so is each kiss,
utterly innocent but oozing with the essence of Divinity
vagabonds gypsies mystics & shamans
have long known the joys
of making love to Source with their souls.
That's why they are always misunderstood
by the masses leading lives of ~quiet-desperation~
If tears were made of ink
I'd use them to write out the meaning of everything
I'd let rivers flow from infinite depths
washing over the fragility of being alive.
I must admit, Dreaming-Bear is an addict for your love
every time I feel your soul smile something Wild in me roars!
That's where the real poetry is at,
in the people, in the moment & it's unfolding
swimming in smiles at the sweet release
as the embrace becomes a drum circle of heartbeats,
the tenderness in a hello & goodbye among lovers.
In the midst of revelation,
Meaning makes an introductory appearance,
& we all cannot help but to bow in its awe inspiring presence
curling our toes with joy as our soul's are ever so softly
kissed into consciousness.

Warm Brimming Bowls Full of Light

There is Light dripping down the innocence of our chin,
collecting into pools of pure potential on the floor of this moment
Saying: breathe through me,
be the wind bursting from my every cell & pore.
The Lover is always saying: come on baby, let's play,
come to the tree of laughter with me
& hand pick a luminous loving thought,
God is our glowing neon fruit hanging
from every branch & limb of this verse & heart.
There are ancient vines in your mind stretching to the top tress
of the Beloved's braided brilliance
that is always so full of giggling galaxies
& softly exploding supernova stars.
Give me your every tear, pain, insecurity, & fear,
in the cauldron of the Lover's kiss,
swimming in the shimmering patience & playfulness of prayer.
Let's make a soup of the soul without all our stories of suffering,
our lifetimes lived in shame & fear.
I'll season your edges with compassion, I'll mix you in with forgiveness
& flame roast you over the fires of freedom
until your simmering to become one with the Sun.
Then my dear, I'll serve you back to yourself
as warm brimming bowls full of contagious happiness.
That way we can both have breakfast in bed with the moment,
as we reminisce about the wordlessness,
when we first found ourselves rising in-love
with the sacred significance of Source.
Our every breath since then,
has been bursting with awareness & holy bewilderment
with every mischievous molecule of our blessed existence,
of having tasted first-hand the star-fruit of the friend.
This is what happened when we tripped face first into the sky,
after having leapt into the oceans of each other's laughter
in gestures of uncontrollable shine-smiling,
as the luminous essence of Love becomes a living Light source
dripping down the innocence of our chin,
collecting into pools of pure potential on the floor of this moment
Saying: breathe through me,
be the wind bursting from my every cell & pore.

Melt in Each Other's Mouth

Right now, I am planting Light in your sweet tender holy heart
sewing my poetic solar-seed into the fertile soil of your soul.
When you awake from this dream
you will discover that all your overwhelming sorrows
have become an orchard of stars,
giving you a billion blooming reasons to smile
& shed all those tears in place of moon-shine
In this very moment, two mermaids
are tickling each other's fire-tenders with their tongues
as they laugh & play in turquoise dreams
upon a luminous emerald laughing sea called your heart.
At night, I lean my face into the skylight,
& let the Lover's kiss reacquaint me with the wild nature of the dark.
I become intoxicated by the Night's lips
pressed quietly against the breasts of the Milky Way.
Who keeps letting out love-release sighs of:
oh my goodness, & wow!
which turn into shooting stars & flaming meteorites
as soon as the words leap from our tongue & thoughts.
We're all pieces of chocolate, some dark, some light
better to curl up close & melt in each other's mouths.
Never a dull moment when you're with Dreaming-Bear my dear,
always something tender to soothe your weeping ear.
In this bed of belonging there's always room for one more,
we'll just all squeeze in a little closer, a little closer,
closer still, squeeze all the way into me,
until we quietly become One heart
beating in rhythm to the sounds of creation
happening in the music of Movement & Light
dancing in tandem with divinity in the dark.
Right now, you are becoming a wild holy flame
poised upon the tip of the tongue of the Tender-One
In this very moment, you are saying what God wants to say,
thinking her soft glowing compassion filled thoughts.
Tell the world my Dear, tell them each & every one,
of just how much we have always been IN-Love like this
with the light we feel in each other's kiss
filling our solar plexus heart space
with a billion joyful suns.

Words Spun into Light

A beautiful moment is always a dangerous realization
that the Beloved has a secret, it's called: Happiness,
& laughter is the Source.
So dissolve my dear, disappear yourself into a sweet tender smile
that is always saying in that beautiful Light language
what every soul needs & longs to hear most
things like: My God you're beautiful!
& don't you know how much I love you?!
For it happens from time to time,
that a Soul hungry enough to become a holy-beggar,
will begin collecting radiance in their bowl,
& then go on wild drinking binges of divinity
getting drunk on the goodness of God
& become so sweet & mischievously amorous in their love,
that they can most often be found
standing outside the Lover's window at night
howling love-laced-lunacy to Source.
Once, on a particularly drunken evening,
Dreaming-Bear joined forces with the Moon & Stars
& tricked the Beloved into braiding us into her hair
now some part of this heart has become the flame
that lights this pale shadow Source we call the Sun
& I kiss this ecstatic spinning world with words
woven into Light filled love-spells.
Feel happiness my Dear, feel beautiful-loving-free & kind
for its thoughts felt with passion that the Universe responds to as prayer
& each of us will ultimately become
what we think & feel ourselves to be most.
With this dangerous realization,
make wanton love to the moment
have your way with reality, & dissolve my Dear,
disappear yourself into God's beautiful-holy-laughter
& become that flame of fascination
that helps to light up the darkened corners
of every broken heart.

The Promised Land

I see you've broken out of your royal cage in the Night's sky,
now my dear, you can finally lay your immortal Love at Light's feet.
See what happens when a heart breaks
see what happens when Love gets broken
it finally finds a way to be completely & utterly open,
shattered like that,
it becomes free of every concept & form
in this divine annihilation we become One,
& find ourselves to be infinite & everywhere.
We are the promised land we've been looking for our whole lives.

Bliss Bread

Kamikaze kisses from the lips of the Holy-One
keep leaping from the tip of the Lover's tongue
& dive bombing my heart in tiny explosions of Laughter & soft Light
breaking new ground inside my thoughts,
turning me inside out so that all I am is a throbbing star,
exposing the softness of this soul
as I share with you my most tender sacred aching parts.
Love is a prayer passing between the Beloved's breath & ours
letting in constellations of compassion as lips do what hands cannot
a tango with tenderness & truth dancing in trinity with our tongues.
In this union, we wed ourselves to freedom
transforming the vibration of our words
into wildly spinning worlds of wonder & bewilderment,
because when we kiss like this Wild Child,
in the heat of the moment, it feels like a holy act of worship
coaxing God to come out & play from her firmament of fantasy,
teasing her to manifest as the tickle we feel
when playing Tag with the innocence of our tongues,
softly saying: you're IT!.
We are Bliss-Bread,
savor the flavor my dear,
don't waste a single crumb of light
let's become kamikaze kisses, & keep throwing bits of our souls
into each other's playful laughing mouths at night.
O let's become each other's favorite midnight snack,
& sneak off while the whole world is dreaming,
& dissolve ourselves into the sacred
parched palette of Love's ecstatic heart.

Love is Dangerous

We've have fire, wind, rain,
& now we've have the earth of each other
sounds like a good beginning to me.
The integration of the moment with our dreams,
the warmth of holding hands & being held
be my cave, & let the bear in me curl up in you & hibernate.
Your body sounds like a tree voicing itself in the night
right now, your breath is my blanket,
covering up this nakedness in the dark.
Sure love is dangerous
many of the best things in life sometimes are,
but if we didn't run the risk of losing ourselves completely,
then what would be the point?
Love has turned me into a rogue genie whenever the moon is full.
What if Romeo & Juliet hadn't spent all night together,
talking & kissing until the sun came up?
They'd have lived longer lives, but then again, who would care?
That's the story no one wants to read.
Because more important than how we die,
is how we have lived,
so, be the deity of my idolatry,
& long after our hearts have stopped beating,
the echoes of this kiss will still be felt
in the pulse of young lovers whose blood boils
with reckless self-abandon
towards the bliss of becoming One.

Let's Dream

Welcome to the playground of the heart
where kisses are our favorite food,
and the stars are our best blanket.
No need for money here,
the only currency is an exchange of touches
given in honor of diametrical desire.
We can be here now for a reason
because God wanted us to meet
& be inside each other like only dreamers can
in a way that is without boundaries.
There is no end to the happiness of our skin
or the sunrise setting in our eyes,
and so we'll let laughter be our language
let it guide us through the secrecy of our stolen moments.
Before we rush off to waking up, let's rise awhile longer,
let's bathe ourselves in sparkling comet tails
& walk on those other shores,
where neither fear nor guilt has tread.
Let's be each other's only weakness,
and find some strength in that.
by building ourselves a home there
made of kindness and love.
We can have any adventure your heart desires
Take my hand,
Make a wish
and let's dream.

Love Spells in a Kiss

How do you say goodnight to someone who isn't even there?
You don't, you just drift off to the forest to dream yourself to sleep
unless you find the One your looking for,
& then of course, nothing says sweet-surrender like a kiss.
In fact, everything that can't be said with words
is voiced in that pink-pressing of flesh.
For every touch whether tender or torrid,
carries with it the intentions of the heart.
What are my lips saying as they gently caress your inner ear?
I am saying: let's drown ourselves in a sea of self-annihilation
& be re-discovered in each other's arms as a heartfelt embrace
belong to me in as much as I have always belonged to you
recognize yourself in Me, for I am your own voice,
echoing off the beat of this heart.
There is so much I want to say to you,
but none of it can be uttered with words
so instead, I give you love spells in a kiss.

The Light of a Billion Suns

Discarded dreams & lost love lay scattered
all along the 'path to enlightenment'
in the valley where the horizon kisses the shore,
sunsets look like God's candlelight,
& our souls are moths drawn to the flame.
The poem of You back-dropped by the sky,
like a saint of mercy smiling in the fading half-light
Lumerian-eyed-angel, heart pounding in the night
teach me to write Love in the clouds where you spill your dew,
so that we can softly explode into rainbows & stars.
Tell me how & where to kiss your hurts,
so that my lips may know the boundlessness of belonging.
What a thing to behold,
the silhouette of Spirit peeking through your skin,
like an ancient remembrance of alchemy & magic.
Flesh of my flesh, blood of my bones,
I am ecstatic over the happiness of being a Poet
in love with living the Poem.
One day our molecules will kiss with complete abandon,
in utter madness & loss of sanity, in the hopes of tasting true love.
I have seen the light of a billion suns,
but none so great as the light that is within.
Flaming-Phoenix come to carry me home
back to the starlit night,
back to the swaying forest of dancing-trees,
back to belonging to the music being sung by the wild Wind's wandering!
My soul knows no better home than to be held in the arms of the Beloved
to feel the breath of the One rise & fall in you, to know at last,
that your heartbeat pounds out the rhythm of God's favorite tambourine.
We are cups of wine in the hands of a wild Hindu goddess,
whose only desire is to make love to Source
with her divine & determined dance of darkness & light.
The formless eye is always open,
ever searching the soul of existence for signs of the Lover,
who has left a trail of kisses
in every atom, wave, & particle of everything
in all dimensions.

100 Proof Wines of Awareness

Come back to the womb with me for just a tickle in time
as we float upon our backs in the pupil of Love's eye.
You make the sweetest mermaid as you dive & play
with holy-bewilderment upon the whirling winds of wonder.
I can hear the Mother's pulse happening all around us
as her blood rushes along in veins of red-dirt-earth.
We can do weightless summersaults & back flips
as we swim naked in a sea of smiles laughing out-loud with passion
as the landscape unfolds to a radiant display of light & color
thrown across the sky in super slow motion.
I have drunk deep from the cup of our togetherness,
soon to discover that the moment had been spiked
with the 100 proof wines of awareness!
The voice of the Oneness whispers soft in my ears,
as a wordless utterance in a symphony of harmonic frequency & vibration
We are baby Buddha on a playground of pure potentiality.
All that we could ever hope to say
is being voiced by the silence of the dark,
in the whisper of leaves & firefly's dreams
within the chanting of crickets
as they beckon forth divinity
from beneath the leaves.

Surrender Everything to Love

Dreaming-Bear has a question for you Wild-Child.
Do you think the caterpillar even remotely comprehends
the enormity of its transformation into a butterfly?
From mundane to magnificent in a matter of moments.
Perhaps the cocoon is the womb they create
to intentionally dream themselves
into something beautiful-free & brand-new.
Let this forest of freedom be our cosmic chrysalis
as we surrender ourselves to Source,
until we emerge from this wilderness of wonder
ready to soar upon rainbow wings!
Along this trail, our tears become turquoise seas
as we tickle each other into ecstasy.
Our hearts kiss, & the stars look like tiny parts of the Moon
that have broken off in a slow-motion explosion,
but when the clouds sleep in late,
the Sky becomes a vast Dream-Catcher made of intersecting galaxies,
& we are cosmic water sparkles
shimmering in the great spiral web of infinity.
Tonight the Universe is the Lover's navel,
& I find myself running through the forest naked exclaiming:
I surrender! I surrender,
I surrender everything to Love!

Playgrounds of Possibility

If we listen closely to the voice that speaks to us in the silence
We can hear everything that can't be said only intimated & felt.
Love scatters her word seed upon the wind
& tosses prayers into the void,
knowing that someday each one shall return
as a secret whispered in the breath of a Lover's sigh of release,
when kissing the playground of Possibility's pounding heart.
Pure-One, I understand the pain you feel
& why you have yet to mend those still bleeding wounds of yours
because your sadness will not allow you to let go
of addictions to being a victim.
But tip your once wounded heart cup close to this hot honey mouth
& let me pour healing sounds
inside your well-spring capacity for forgiveness,
for when you drink from the freedom of that fountain,
everything dissolves into a voice from wilderness.
your fears & regrets are forced to confess
that all they ever were was a hoax,
& their masquerade was really just child's play
upon the emotional merry-go-round of your heart's theme park.
Along with all the other unwanted & unclaimed vulnerabilities
you've sheltered in the secrecy of yourself for so long
that you can't remember anymore where Love came from or how.
Even as emotional pranksters play parlor tricks with your pain,
tease them back with the tickle of tender forgiveness,
run wide-armed to each one who has hurt you
embrace them as you would your guru,
grateful for the gift of an opportunity to learn through the tears.
Greet your so called enemies with a Hug & kiss like lovers do,
to set them free from their seeming separation.
Let all your parts dance wild & unashamed
upon the wind of your soul's imagination wandering
back to the playgrounds of possibility
where every moment is also an invitation
drawing us closer to the vibrant pursed lips of the Beloved,
who is the very presence of the voice
that speak to us in the silence.

The Soul of Truth

We are angels of Darkness & Light,
born to embody a brand-new existence of laughter & love,
of vulnerability & pain, of honest heartfelt gratitude
towards the beauty & brilliance of the Beloved.
We can play hide & seek in each other's dreams
as we hold hands & run knee-high through a field of stars
I love the way lovers lips dance,
each kiss is a tiny explosion of tenderness & desire,
each touch a remembrance of the softness of ourselves
in the skin of one another,
the symphony of our breath dancing wild & untamed with the wind!
What I have discovered in the pages of you
is a truth more valuable & lasting than all the scriptures
of all the religions of the world.
I want you to be free Wild-Love,
free of resentment, blame, & suffering sorrow
I want you to know the freedom & ecstatic happiness of pure being.
I want you to know this love of mine,
which is without condition, & that says in the silence:
be as you are Wild-Flower, beautiful & blossoming
in absolute surrender to the magic of the moment.
Look into these tiger's-eyes filled with angel's-tears,
& tell me that you can see the turquoise sparkles spiraling.
Walk with me along the pathless path
& let us blaze together a new trail to the soul of Truth.
I want to give our heart wings,
so that we can know the completion of being One with the Sky
then, like stars, we'll burn & spin in the orbit of each other,
until our thirst for discovery is satisfied,
& then we can fall together in the freedom of the night,
while young lovers make whishes upon our tail spin…
& we disappear in the dark wordless wonder
of the One.

What It's Like To Kiss God

This is what it's like to kiss God
a pair of butterflies seducing each other in the Sun,
the laughter of the river as it tickles the rocks
a single tear rolling down the cheek of innocence,
the deep breath in, followed by an exhale of I Love You
baby's giggles bouncing off mother's breast,
the look in lover's eyes when they finally find one another across time
a whisper of wind caressing the back of your neck,
the sound of a feather as it softly slices the air
a dragonfly's daydreams
being held tightly by the one you love the most,
moonlight making love to the ocean
comets colliding & careening through the universe,
the dance of light & water reflecting off your soul
two clouds coming together to form one divine passion of sky,
the sounds of playgrounds echoing in your ears
the mad rush & exhilaration of knowing & being known,
holding hands in secret when no one else is looking
the freedom of falling & the softness of being caught,
the drum circle of heartbeats that happens in every hug
holding & being held,
the sound of the Friend's voice caressing your ear
coming home to the warm eager embrace of the Beloved,
knowing who you really are at last
& finally knowing what you have to do,
& finally, knowing
what you have to do.

Love-affair of Water & Light

Each conversation is also a love-song of light
expressing itself in the music & commune-ication
of being self-aware in this sacred symphony of Oneness.
There is a scripture of uniqueness in each grain of sand
spelling out the softness in the lips of the Lover.
Look at your reflection in the river, know forever
that you are a living love-affair of Water & Light,
making-out in the form of flesh,
& deeper than that you are composed of starlight's desire
to be ambient & in-love.
Meet me at sundown over the Ridge
where we can whisper crazed love-poems
in each other's always amorous ears
about our most intimate moments spent laughing wildly
in the arms of the One.
A band of 300,000 angels has gathered themselves
upon glistening shores in the corners of our mouth,
to hear the torrid details of our dance with Divinity
in the darkness of womb-light.
They've built campfires & pitched tents,
diving in & out of our words
embodying everything we say,
searching for signs of the recognition of awareness
that comes from having been utterly ravished
by the Devastating-Beauty.
All have gathered, to hear what we'll say
about loving God as each other!
Something so undeniable & full of self-sacrifice,
because every enlightened being
has voluntary chained themselves to the will of Love.
Laughter is born for no reason at all
in the spontaneity of the Moment,
& contrary to popular belief,
there is no doorman in Heaven checking names,
(for heaven has no doors) all are welcomed in with open arms,
everyone gets forgiven of everything in the end.
Although some may still find it amusing

to imagine different kinds of 'hell'
as a way of teasing themselves with imaginary fears,
but if I'm wrong Wild-Love, we can always dig a 'tunnel' to heaven
& sneak ourselves inside with the tenderness of a Kiss
see, the Lover has already left a key to her presence
under our Heart's welcome-matt, & secret love-letter which reads:
welcome home my Love, climb the stars to my bed-chamber with prayer,
I'll be ready & perfectly willing
to fulfill your every desire, dream, & longing.

Come Ravish Me

As the sun sets where the river-children still laugh & play,
dragonflies gather by the thousands to dance
with those million tiny sparkles making love to the water with Light.
Dreaming-Bear has some wild honey to share with you Beautiful-One,
because something sweet to say always speaks to our soul
& makes every single moment just a little more tender.
The Beloved & I are very close personal friends,
so I feel I can share with you
a few of her deepest quirky secrets:
every night as she gets ready to dream,
she lays herself upon the softest clouds,
shakes stars from her hair,
& takes the Moon off like an ear-ring
which she lays upon the mantle
of her intergalactic bedside fireplace
unfolds the blossoming louts of her heart
to reflect the Sun's goodnight kiss,
then crossing her fingers for luck,
the last thing she says
every night before she dreams,
is your sweet name…
followed by this incantation:
come to me Wild Love,
come ravish my heart with laughter & prayers!

An Irresistible Invitation To Belong

The flowers in the garden are fragrant & pure,
but it's the ones growing wild that really make us high!
Nothing is as free & untamed as the wind
which is the Beloved's breath kissing the softness of our skin.
Today the Sun has followed me everywhere I go,
dancing in sparkles upon water, peeking at me through the trees,
like a childhood friend whose smile is always so full of Light
reminding me that shadows of suffering will come & go,
& even the darkest desperation is also temporary,
for everything eventually evolves into the tenderness of Love's glow.
I have risen so in-love with the Oneness,
that I often discover myself passionately reciting love poems
out loud to inanimate objects,
which have neither ear to hear nor tongue to reply,
because some part of me knows that the Lover is always Present,
within each particle of everything in existence
just waiting to be noticed in the nothingness of being,
that somehow also encompasses being All.
The challenge Dear-One is to see beyond all this seeming separation,
that has angels & devils flying on different wings
but in the same semantic circles of misunderstanding & answered prayers.
The illusion completes itself in vivid specificity,
with elaborate attention paid to every detail,
a masterpiece of matter to disguise that which Matters most.
But the magic of mystery is no slight of hand, no parlor tricks here
it's a spell as simple as being a seed planted in the soil of the soul,
given the water of wisdom & the light of joy,
the seed must decide how & when to grow.
There is no destination outside oneself
to satisfy all the begging questions,
who scream like starving children
desperate for the milk of meaning & acknowledgment.
But the breasts of God are always bare,
& dripping with a drink of divinity.
Mother's milk is made of laughter & mischief
commingling with an overwhelming sense of beauty
in this cocktail of consciousness
where every kiss exists
as an irresistible invitation to belong.

In The Arms of The Beloved

Down by the lotus pond where Krishna plays his flute
for Radha's sweet kiss
the reflection on the water is a universe of discovery,
& lovers sneak off into the forest
to offer themselves as prayers upon the altar
of each other's playful pounding hearts.
One can practice the path of 'enlightenment' to achieve Buddha-hood,
but who will go to explore the pathless voice of the wilderness
that contains as yet undiscovered truth that the old prophets never knew?
Who will make-out with the Mystery in the form of new discovery,
& rise so in-love with Source that they disrobe themselves
of every concept & form?
Peace & Passion are playing tug-of-war
with the emotional strings of your heart,
while Ego & Reason stand on the side-lines laughing,
each time someone falls over the line,
they all embrace wildly & tickle each other with a kiss exclaiming:
Instant Winner!
Reach inside your soul & take out a handful of stars,
you can wrap the Moment in them as a gift of being present.
Take a break Dear-One from all your labors of separation,
for Dreaming-Bear knows it is the heaviest burden you carry in this world
to think that you are not always being warmly embraced
in the sweet merciful arms of Love.

Stars in Her Stare

In the mini movie-theater of your mind
stars gather to applaud an encore viewing
of the Beloved's surrendering of herself to the Moment's many forms.
Let anyone who is hurting sit by the rush of these words
for a soft revelation to accompany your hearts quietly pounding drum.
Today Love's eyes are filled with a pilgrimage of cascading clouds,
expressing themselves tenderly in every direction,
while butterflies spin in ecstasy
in the shafts of sunlight kissing the tops of trees.
Tonight, they'll be stars in her stare mixed with moons
and a whole galaxy of cosmic cousins
dancing wildly in the dark-conscious-chaos.
Rivers sing songs of understanding our sadness,
with water-like laughter elbowing the sides of rocks
while lovers dream of what it will one day mean
to turn themselves into tears that flow freely
like river-words that merge to become One in the ocean of God's heart.
Come close My Dear, & let me tickle your ear with softly spoken secrets
on why the Mantis prays & Dragonflies dream
in the glowing pools of light where the Goddess goes to bathe.
The skin of these words has been jasmine-kissed
by the wind of the Lover's breath,
leaning in close to make-out with existence
in the form of softly merging with the laughter & pain
happening deep within the soul of this world of matter & meaning.
If you'll let me, I can turn on a secret light
in your Heart's most ancient forgotten chamber,
where Source keeps all her truest priceless treasures of Mystery,
each of which she has tucked away in you,
to be expressed as a living masterpiece of fascination.
Don't kill your unborn dreams with maybe's & what if's
for they are the children of Potential
which you nurture with kindness & a kiss,
who will eventually give birth to your irrevocable bliss
& have your thoughts forever dancing intimately with the Friend.
I have written so many love-poems in your honor
that the Moon dared to take away my pen in a fit of jealousy,

after I accidentally admitted that her sweet kiss
always reminds me of softly glowing with you.
Fairy's wings & falling stars, that's what magic is made of,
I have a handful of each to toss into the cauldron of dreams,
which will turn us both into gently rising prayers.

You Made a Promise

Come be my Golden Angel, my open Door of Light
let me settle my Soul between your shoulder blades
until the breath of these words softly becomes wings.
The Universe is constantly expanding, so why shouldn't we?
The Truth is: ~we Are the living water that Christ spoke of~
literally, we are aquifers of the Amorous-One's soul of liquid-light.
Come close & I will spoon feed you brilliant bites of God,
in between exhales of ecstasy & love poems filled with the wine of prayer,
which rise like incense & greet your ancient Heart's appetite for Devotion.
Somewhere along the way from being born naked & free,
to where you are now, someone managed to convince you
that you were less than you really are.
But why keep your Mind chained to a beast of burden
who keeps dragging you along through the fields of 'have-to & obligation'
why not trade in your stockpile of the mundane
which you have been collecting your whole life?
Exchange it all for a this magic moment of magnificence
that will multiply & manifest meaning
to unshackle you from all your addictions to suffering & pain.
In the beginning, before you were formed,
you made a promise to yourself & the world, which you have yet to keep.
You said, in front of & along with every soul in existence:
~I vow to remember my purpose
& live a life that reminds everything of its beauty~
Now, it is all Dreaming-Bear can do
but to keep quietly repeating with my every sacred breath:
~Let me be One with Source, take me Home, let me be One with You~
so close that I feel you happening in every heartbeat,
so deep that you become the breath in these lungs
filling up with Love.

Everything Becomes God Again

I keep getting dreams caught in my hair
& tenderness tangled between breaths
as I hold hands with Love & make out with God as the moment!
Pretty soon, all our sorrows will also become all our joys
as we recognize the Lover softly kissing over the fragility of everything.
Life is an invitation to be loving & kind
The best teachers never stop being students,
so let's see what we can learn from a deeply felt press of lips,
rub navels with eternity,
& let me be in you now along with all things Dreaming.
If I die today in your arms let me be reborn tonight in your heart
as an unmitigated act of compassion.
The Great-Oneness has made love to us all,
drowning in a pool of divine desire inside ourselves & each other.
The question isn't "what can't we be"
the real question is: "what haven't we been?"
We were once One with everything in existence,
who's to say we won't be that way again
even as we already are, even as we have always been.
I bow to everything as my Beloved,
because everything becomes God again
in the end.

Whirling Dervish of Wind

The Beloved concluded her lessons on Love by saying:
In acknowledging our smallness
we can then look to our unrealized-greatness,
& once in our Greatness,
the lesson then becomes to remember our Oneness.
Dreaming-Bear asked: Why were we born?
Source responded: we are here to experience the contrast,
Between being infinite energy & finite beings
to heal the hurting & broken,
because We know what it means to be a fragmented whole.
We were born to be a conduit of Love & to be aware of it
for, if we allow ourselves feel into everything,
we can sense from the farthest reaches of the Multi-verse
to the deepest cosmic inner-verse & every dimension in between.
We are vast & unending & everything will make sense again
once you hear the music of what an instrument your Soul can be.
For there are thousands of tiny symphonies
happening inside your skin with each rise & fall of breath
we are the whirling-dervish of wind.
Dreaming-Bear then asked:
So in the sound the hurricane, what are we really hearing?
The Beloved replied:
That my dear, is the softest utterance
of the Lover's lips whispering our names.

Indescribable Beauty

Look into the mirror of these words
until you softly become the poem looking back.
With one foot in fidelity & one foot in freedom,
Fascination takes a free-fall dive
from the top of your Soul's head to the bottom of the Beloved's feet.
When something goes wrong & everything seems to fall apart,
Love whispers this invitation in the inner-ear of your heart saying:
~Trust Me Dear-One… Trust Me~
for you are always in my deepest awareness.
Preferences are but premeditated resentments in this game of give & take
which we play with our joy because everyone appears to be addicted
to proving their point & having to always be 'right'
just so the ego can finally feel exonerated of its mistakes.
But why look for imaginary diamonds in the dark,
when the Lover has already gift-wrapped the Moment for our pleasure?
God loves us so much, that she has cut off tiny slivers of her own soul
as the price for all this having a body & pretending to be separate.
There is no religious rite of passage or physical feat of greatness
that can make us any more or less deserving,
or bring us closer to understanding the experience of Love.
Its an internal act of worship as simple as letting go of the rope of reason
which we've used to climb our way to where we are now
on the continuum of consciousness, & allowing ourselves to rise,
in wide-eyed wonder, out of control, with complete abandon
to rise so dangerously in-Love with Source,
that you dissolve effortlessly into everything
& let yourself disappear in the indescribable beauty
of your own glowing giggling heart.

The After-Life of Light

Say a sweet prayer with Dreaming-Bear
& let's be consumed by the seduction of Source.
come alive with me in the night
& we can discover what it truly means to be Spirit made Flesh!
We touch, & stars fall from their cradle
amazed at the awareness designed in our fingertips
swirling universes made of soft spiral lines in skin.
We are children of Night shimmering sweetly in the forest of light
if we so desire it, this whole galaxy of stars
would pour themselves into our mouths as mother's milk,
so let's dive deep & swim together in the lake of laughter,
for there are discoveries waiting for us in those divine depths
moments so wordless & bespeaking of beauty,
& what we are really saying to each other in the silence is:
~I honor you, I honor you, I honor you~
Float-dance with me back up to the tops of tree's dreams
swaying softly in the night like a great big-green lullaby.
Curl up close with me like a moth gets acquainted with the flame,
as we become One with God & burn,
in the morning, which is the after-life of Light,
we grow, we transform, we change.

When Words Become Worlds

Life is a double entendre, a meaning within a Meaning.
Love, in Her infinite wisdom, spoke words to create worlds
& Dreaming-Bear in kind, with these love spells
tries what must seem the most infinitesimal effort to do the same.
Painting pictures with the potency of pure potential.
If these Words are an extension of this soul,
living love spells as creations unto themselves,
Could it be, that we are the same? Another of God's love-songs
an expression of some abstract quantum thought
She chose to give Life by reciting us out loud,
or by thinking of beauty & then dreaming us into being.
These line drawings are bits and pieces of this soul
& that is what we are, a little of Love's mind, the peace of Her heart,
a poetic expression of the way She was feeling
on the day life delivered us.
We are the paradigm of Oneness expressed to the utmost extent,
living breathing examples of Light's point of view.
Now to see through the eyes of Love, & write with Her Divine penmanship,
bringing to life the latent potential swimming within our Imagination.
How fascinating, Words creating Life, Life creating Poetry
Poetry creating Worlds.

A Lush for Love

The moment is pregnant & giving birth through this page
these words are children running with laughter
through your heart's playground.
This Wild-Love within us all is growling-deep,
hungry for a glimpse of the Glowing-One,
ravenous for a taste of her honey-filled mouth.
So I undressed my sweetest sacred-intent
& kissed right through the veil of illusion
with one thought of uncontrollable joy!
& what I saw on the other side was utterly wordless but entirely felt.
That is to say, I saw God dancing,
like people do in front of their mirror
or when they think no one else is looking, with abandon & happiness
wearing nothing but an ecstatic expression
of complete compassion & pure-contentment.
As if to say: leave all your doubts behind my Dear
for this verse will one day kiss the heart-lips of the world with tenderness
dancing Light diving off the tip of your thought's tongue
& into the vast seas of the Soul's sweet spot.
Now I have become a connoisseur of Divine-Wines,
I am a Lush for Love!
Savoring each of the Beloved's many barrels
of fermented laughter & tears
which she keeps hidden in your heart's catacombs.
In my drunkenness I have grabbed the Universe as my pen,
& I write these words with fire upon the pages of your very heart,
so that when darkness comes, you'll shine like softly smiling stars.
The Moon is our playground, the solar system is our backyard
if we hop this flimsy fence of forgetting,
we will see that every moment is Holy,
& in each sacred breath we are only a poem's width away
from kissing the lips of Love, we are always only a heartbeat away
from making out with God in prayer.

Cup of Light

There is a river of radiance rushing from the mountain peak pages
upon the soft inner core undulating as your luminous oceanic soul.
Come Pure-One, let us share this cup of Light
let us pour something of ourselves & stars
into the cauldron of each other's playful spinning hearts.
Just as Thought must dissolve to become a Kiss,
so does Wood whisper a confession in Fire's ear saying:
consume me, every part, let me change & disappear into Oneness,
let me become a visible prayer & be vaporized in the Sky.
Tonight they'll be a tribe of ten-thousand laughing drunken angels
camped out in the curve & crevice of your pillows
they've gathered to witness first hand the painfully-beautiful
sweet-sadness of watching you once again torture yourself
with thoughts of separation from Source,
hoping to one day see you free your essence of entanglements
to every shrine of guilt our minds & this world has erected.
Come Dear-One, let us share this cup of Light
for you I have milked drops of the Sun
into each of these holy-hand-written worlds,
so that you might begin to heal every wound
& dissolve every concept or form anyone every taught you about Love.
For you I have cried golden-tears to use as ink,
so that God can be sprawled out in Liquid-Light
drowning every eager inch of your eyes & this page.
If you come close to this inspired Uni-Verse Dear-One,
if you come closer still…
so close that these prayers become your thoughts,
then the Lover will reach out of this book
grab your soul by the shirt of the body,
& kiss you with complete divine abandon.
But beware my Shining-Friend,
for just one glance from the Love's lips
is enough to turn even the most disenchanted of believers
into compassion-crazed lunatics
who keep offering this dry world a drink
from the luminous cups
of their own glowing heart.

A Drink of Each Other

Let's become water & merge our rivers
into One overflowing ocean of the unknown
surely there are depths there that deserve to be explored,
like touching tattoos in the darkness
tracing the outline of your soul with my index finger
playing the instrument of each heartbeat & breath,
what sweet music we become when we're in harmony with ourselves
as Love begins to make us from the clay of its own heart.
If kissing God were a crime then I'd be guilty on all charges
& would gladly surrender myself to the consequence of being free.
Out here in the Wild, every tree has a face,
& if we look at them through the eyes of our heart
then we will see that each one is a wooden reflection of our own.
So while the world is watching
let's give them a moment they can never forget
something sacred & utterly exploding with the divinity of purpose,
something as egoless & sincere as a heartfelt embrace
a glancing of the lips, a naked unfolding of vulnerability.
For you, I will slice pages from the night
to fasten stars upon with needle & thread,
sewing a seed of light to spell out the darkness
filled with scattered dreams & misplaced prayers.
Timelessness will tell the story of our togetherness across lifetimes
of how our every embrace was also a poem & a prayer,
of how we discovered God sleeping in our navels
& tickled her to come out & play in the night of our youth
of how we never gave up but were always willing to surrender
to the willingness to become tenderness.
At the very least my Love, if we become water,
then we can quench our overwhelming thirst for the Beloved
with a drink of each other.

The Dreaming-Tree

The woods are my sanctuary,
the Dreaming-Tree my temple
the Earth, my home.
My favorite parts of existence are the looks in peoples eyes,
the transformation in their hearts,
& the undeniable recognition that something truly beautiful is happening.
It is a story of remembering our ancient past,
& resurrecting some dormant part of who we once were,
it's about Love… true unconditional Love
it's a deep unmitigated pain & overwhelming sorrow,
like catching angels tears in buckets.
It's a song of forgiveness & freedom from fear
a naked dance covered in earth & laughter.
It's an honoring of the mother, & embracing of the father,
like looking across the room
& seeing how beautiful all the other you's really are.
It's a Great-Oneness being spoken by the wind,
an invitation to join in the recreation of reality!
Sometimes I walk through the woods
smiling out-loud with laughter & tears,
amazed & grateful for the dream my life has become.
Seducing Shaman's & mesmerizing medicine-people,
kissing each other into consciousness with words that become worlds,
& songs that serenade the heart strings of spirit.
What happens when you challenge the world to be as beautiful as it can be,
simply by being the most beautiful You?
Then things will never be the same.
Let there be but one conviction of complete & utter thoughtfulness,
practiced in sincere gestures of compassion & kind action
let us offer up prayers that are free of religious lace,
prayers for the hurting & the broken,
for those suffering else where & here at home
prayers uttered from that deepest most sacred part of our Soul.
Let us find some comfort there among the harmony of held hands,
of personal drum-circles happening in the form of hugs.
When our hearts connect like that, through the intimacy of our chests,
they pound out a rhythm of hello & goodbye.

We are a sacred symmetry of tightly embracing universes,
coming together to create a new dimension of meaning.
When the moon is full,
I drift off through the forest of Grandmother-kissed leaves,
& climb these roots saying:
the woods are my sanctuary,
the Dreaming-Tree my temple
the Earth, my home.

Darkness Made Light!

It's a different language being spoken by the flowers & trees,
one that can't be talked with your tongue,
only whispered with the Soul
where everything is undulating in Love's Light,
in slow-motion gravity-defying waves of ambient musical Oneness.
My heart is an ocean filled with bioluminescent dolphins,
& out of the depths rises the flaming-blue-sea-turtle.
Your smile is a thousand sunsets in multicolor all at once!
Let's cover up in a cocoon made of fulfilling potential of our heart,
& transform ourselves into creatures of new thought.
Pain is the womb, & light is laughter being born
as we perform the alchemy of presence
& transform darkness into light.

The Pleasure & Pain of So Much Belonging

Like a child with a perpetually new toy,
so is the Lover's lips to the Beloved.
I feel you blossoming in the flower of your youth,
the stars I see in your eyes are a pair of twin-universes,
that compliment the sunrise of your smile.
I have lost all sense of inhibition, & defied every convention
to plant myself deeply inside the soil of your soul,
and grow new roots of discovery in the most unspeakable parts..
I am compelled by Love's lessons,
the romantic charm of tenderness & respect.
the way we undress each other's old-wounds,
peeling off layers to get to the Source.
Who has ever been more in love than this?
To know the vast ocean in each teardrop,
& to taste the pleasure & pain
of so much belonging.

Soul-Candy

Wild wet & wind-blown, like a prophet in heat
I prowl through the forest hungry for a kiss from the lips of Love
to leave me languishing in ecstasy & sweet serenity of Source.
Night is the soul of Day undressing itself in the dark
like lovers do, with impassioned prayerful purpose.
The silhouette of laughter
teasing the tickle-spot of a new emotion to awaken & dream.
Come with me to where the fires mate upon moonlit waters
to dissolve & become One with the night sun,
where the mermaids sing existence into being,
& stars take suicide leaps hand in hand off the edge of existence,
just to know the exhilaration of what it means to fall
recklessly into the Great Unknown!
Something golden in me has honesty dripping from these lips like honey;
Love-consciousness is candy for your soul's sweet tooth.
Dreaming-Bear's heart-spring is always overflowing for you,
with something good to drink from the depths of God
water of life flows free
through the blood in the veins of these words.
My prayer for you is that you rise in love
with the magic meaning inherent in everything,
to such a degree that your every action
is also a sweet token of affection
offered in devotion to the One,
with as much consideration as lovers take
upon the night of their union
with quiet heartfelt kisses, ecstatic utterances of joy,
& a tenderness that bespeaks of always belonging.
If you are hurt, know that I will bleed with you,
if you should fall & somehow be broken,
you can use my soul as a bed of healing
to mend yourself whole through the power of dreaming.
These words will be the grass beneath your feet
that tickles the child in you to play hide & seek
in each other's heart-space
Come play with me in our Togetherness Tree
where the wind is a kiss to the land,

blown in from across the Ocean,
we'll laugh & play away all that has gotten shattered.
When you're ready just speak the name,
& love will appear in your most fantastic dreams,
to re-awaken all that is deepest within you,
a voice in the wilderness carried in the rush of the river.
Source is the Lover, we are the Beloved,
both are infinite, both are in love
& in constant need of each other.

An Artist in Love

I sketch you with these words
like an artist in love.
You have been etched
on my heart
forever.

Dreaming-Bear Speaks

When all the world around you rages,
& the worst of what you have imagined comes true
when every back turns, & every eye fails to meet yours,
even if you are being lied about,
& your name dragged through the city sewers
do not walk then in disgrace Wild-One
but hold your head high & look to compassion for companionship.
In a wordless language, the universe says,
I am here, even in your most sorrowful secret sufferings.
Even now these words are mending your wound-weary soul,
let unconditional love lead you home,
where the smiles are as sincere & meaningful as child's hugs,
as holy as lovers lips parted in a kiss of sweet tender affections,
as unashamed & guilt-free as tears falling from innocent eyes.
Out there in the void, those man-made streets of steel & concrete
there are tragedies that even tears cannot describe,
but none so great a mistake as the cruelty of not caring.
Listen with your heart Pure-One,
& know that I am with you in every rise & fall of breath,
in every joy & sorrow,
every laughter & pain that goes unnoticed, this heart says,
we're all broken, just in different ways, & this is how we mend.
To care for the one who seeks to tear you down,
to offer honest heartfelt prayers
for the one who longs for your destruction
to ask with all your being that they be blessed by the Great Oneness,
& to know in the end that though you be wounded
by knives of the thoughtless, they cannot cut you so deep
that Love won't then come & fill that wound
with an overwhelming capacity for transformation of pain into beauty.
Remember who & what you really are,
see yourself & others through the eyes of tenderness,
& know at last, that we are all beautiful in the Heart of God
all will be forgiven of their inconsistencies,
all will be welcomed into the boundlessness of Becoming!
In the end Wild-Love, you cannot be diminished,
you cannot be abandoned or forgotten,

for you are held in the soul of Source,
& one day, when all dualities have dissolved
even your worst enemy will become a part of you,
even as they have always been,
now you can smile & be amused that you have been tortured so
by the wisps of nothing that surround our lives.
I am here with you, in this moment of utter un-certainty,
& wherever you may follow the trails of your heart
know this most of all,
existence is a great wide Unknown
& though you seem lost at times
you are never left alone
Dreaming-Bear is always with you.

Love Spell 4:
An Alternate History
Of The Universe

In the beginning there was Laughter, echoing in the arena of reality, and unreality. Laughter is only a word that I use to describe the beginning, there really is no word in Human for such a thing, but I say laughter because it is the closest description of original form, which was form-less and still is. Laughter laughed so hard and so long that it began to shine, it began to give off life, and from its glow was born the substance that we've come to know as Light. Light is a life form, each particle of light is a life of its own, like people of a conscious community, individuals that glow to give, each separate, yet all radiating from one source, all sentient and aware. Light speaks only one language, that of complete and utter joy. Light knows only one Emotion, pure happiness, contagious! You see, light affects us even if we don't know it, when we laugh, when we feel selfless and holy, it is light passing through us. I'll tell you a secret: Children, are made of light, we all are in the beginning. In fact, everything in its original pristine and most basic form comes from light, and laughter is the mother of light, it is also where light lives, like giggles coming home to become laughs of their own.

Look around you, what do you see? Or should I ask, what do you Think you see? Do you honestly believe that anything visible would still be there without light to make it appear? All that you see and perceive, are particles of light coming together, everything within your sight is only visible because of the desire of light to be Light and alive. It is the reality maker, without it there would be nothing, we owe a debt to light, it is the shape giver, the color maker, without light there'd be no memory of anything, there'd be no beginning, and no end, no coming and going, no knowledge of anything that is or could be. It's true, light is a life form and it shines on Purpose, it exists with intelligent intent, which is a deep-rooted effort to make all things possible. Everything acknowledged, and most things un-acknowledged were invented by different kinds of light coming together and deciding to shine in a certain way, even darkness (the great secret keeper) which I will get to soon, exists as a result of light's longing for contrast.

From light came the birth of Shadows shadows are brother, sister, children to light, and they find their purpose in light's desire to shine. Shadows speak light's language, but unbeknownst to light, shadows live secret lives of their own for they also speak a language which light cannot fully understand, it's called Illusion! This is where amusement begins, you see shadows are playing, and have been playing for all time, the biggest game of copycat in the history of Existence, miming and distorting every move of all things in a sincere effort to make fun of existence, but existence stopped getting the joke long ago, of course, that never stopped them from playing, and when we're not looking, shadows take naps.

After a while of playing practical jokes, shadow and light created a new language they called Mischief, & in that Mystery was born Darkness. Now darkness has gotten a bad rap, it's called evil and fiendish, but the truth is, (and here is another secret for you to tell), there is no Evil, only different degrees of Misunderstanding & there is no Good either, only varying degrees of comfort-ability. Darkness developed as a womb & decorated the inner lining of her heart with Stars, now darkness is the plenum, and was there in the invisible robes of laughter as a yin-yang twin of the light & shadow, it is therefore by definition only a degree of less light & to an extent an even deeper degree of shadow, or to put it plainly, darkness too is conscious alive and wandering. As it turns out, darkness became pregnant with the cosmos, when light, the energetic luminous seed, planted itself in her soul's soil, and shadow was the midwife who helped the mystery give birth to all that was to follow.

Darkness became swollen in a blooming expansion filled with inter-dimensional Multi-verses of conjoined Galactic twinfinities, her first born child she aptly named Nature who in turn would be the big sister to nurture every aspect which was born thereafter. From the birth pangs of this celestial labor, darkness developed Tears, which turned into liquid Consciousness, in the form of Water, worlds, ice comets, interstellar clouds & the raindrops of skin that would ultimately become the very essence of every kind of Life. As darkness birthed it wept, & continued to expand & contract expelling latent potential for billions of light years in every direction along the nomadic moment of movement which evolved into Gravity as a way of bringing all the sentient-siblings back together in harmony.

Elements emanated from the birth of Space-Time to Intention a crib-like container for the new born Creation. Elements are the Magic holders of the world Made! They pulled a molecule sized portion from laughter's invisible robes & fashioned it into the material Reality upon which they allowed enough room for the formation of every contingent causal possibility. Among their many works of art was this cerulean blue planet wherein they Made all manner of self-perpetuating species, the most recent 'random' mutation of Matter which became known as Humanity. Now humans are not what you think we are, we are not this skin and flesh, we are not these blood and bone bio-suits, that came much later, we are in fact something altogether different, we are the skin-thin Genes into which Infinity stuffs her immortal Essence.

You see, humans being born on the trail of tears as it were, abandoned their awareness in exchange for addictions to 'power' & somehow convinced themselves in to being 'separate' & feeling finite (afraid of practically everything that wasn't a part of themselves) humanity beheld existence in all its unlimited potential all its vastness and unbridled expanse. This too scared humans and so they came together and made a pact to Forget, and in order to do so they created something which would change their own understanding of existence, it was called a Limit. Now limits were designed to give humans a sense of control-ability and the belief that there was order to existence, but unexpectedly, limits took on a life of their own, and grew beyond the ability of humanity to control. An example of a limit that we created is this Personality of ours, and its malformed misguided cousin of organized oppression called the Ego or selfish identity.

From the onset of limit's rapid increase, humans found themselves more and more unable to do astral feats which once considered common place, until eventually we became fractions of the boundless beings we'd once been, deceiving ourselves into believing that we are confined to the cell, atom, & molecule, frail and susceptible to everything kind of illusion that can be concocted. When in actuality, these bodies are but bio-suit cocoons from which the under go the metamorphosis of expansion through experience and contrast in the form of karmic contractual agreements we sign before being reborn. One of the veins of limit's evolution was this thing called Can't, and the truth my friend is that there is no such thing as can't, there is only Can, but you wouldn't remember that because of the ~can't-pact~ our originals made so long ago. Now when laughter & light, shadow & darkness saw what humans had done to themselves they knew right away that some remedy must be devised for the effects of duality, and so laughter, the great mother of all decided that it would remind humans of what they'd lost by giving them a gift, which was her crowning self-sustaining achievement and she called it Imagination.

Imagination was designed out of the four aspects that came before everything, & who spoke a common language of Co-creation in order to help out humanity. Imagination is essentially comprised of half of the existence of the quintessence, half of the essence of laughter, half of the essence of light, half of the essence of shadow, and half of the essence of darkness combined to form the entirety of this unbridled Limitlessness, which went then to live within humanity's subconscious, and was intended to give us a chance to become once again what we could still be and what we were, from the beginning . Imagination was intended to help us Remember that there is no such thing as a boundary, and that we can do away with them altogether if we would only use the Power of our internal ingenuity.

Now humans didn't know what to do with imagination at first, and so they created all sorts of things with it, many of which I do not really have time to tell you all about, but sufficed to say that everything that is not a part of this Quatrain of original existers, all things great and small, are a direct result of imagination being used. At first humans only imagined infinitesimally, Thought became Subatomic Particles, who in turn gave birth to molecular creatures of all kinds, and then they began to imagine even greater things like the Multi-verse and the countless eternities that comprise its being. Imagination is the precursor to Manifestation projected holographically, & each Entity, including imagination itself is alive and real, and each gives birth to a thing or things of its own.

Perhaps the saddest and most unrealizable development of all was the forlorn fact that humans, despite this gift which cost so much, could still not overcome this flirtatious addiction to old patterning, we could not let go of our preconceived notions, and our assumptions about life and reality, except for the golden few who somewhere along the way began to listen to the voice of imagination which came at first in the form of Dreams. Now dreams are the emissaries of imagination, & were sent incognito through our sleep to speak to us, because that is when we are most likely to listen, with our brains shut down like that, our hearts remain open, & we feel our way into our infinity, but even dreams though full of discovery, could not convince us to let go entirely of our crippling notions, and humanity spiraled even deeper into itself.

The most ironic thing then happened, something so unpredicted and yet serendipitously delightful at the same time. One of the children of limit created the mother of the thing that would give birth to our salvation and liberation as sentient beings. Limit's favorite child was called Skin, who after a while developed a burning desire to be touched and felt by other kinds of skin, and in that desire was born the Kiss, which is essentially the pressing of two pieces of flesh with Affection, (and here is where the story really gets exciting and begins to get juicy and make sense).

Now kissing gave birth to all kinds of things, but the most prominent, the first, and the most important thing it gave birth to was Love, and love is the exclamation point at the end of this sentient sentence of origins which brings us full circle, because love, my friends, the instant it was born gave birth to triplets: Forgiveness, Kindness, and then unimaginably to a tiny tickle she named: Laughter, which is the mother of all, and which is where all things come from and end up in the end again anyway, for when we laugh, we become inextricably intoned with the very heart all of that was, is or ever will be, no longer finite, but formless & free, reabsorbed into the Source where our roots still run deep, & from whence we sprang this blooming being, for this is all happening, has happened, and will happen again in a billion different ways in all times & possible places at once, and it is the Truth, whether anyone acknowledges it or not.

www.dreamingbear.net